CU00673295

Leis
Guide
to the
South West
Coast Path

Minehead to Westward Ho!

Martin Pullen

Also by Martin Pullen

The Completely Useless Guide to London
The Completely Useless Guide to Christmas
The Completely Useless Guide to England

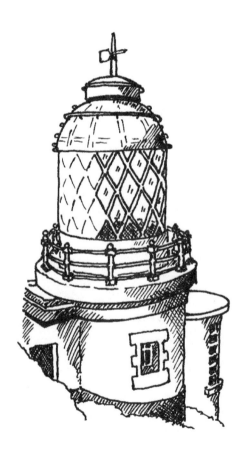

Leisurely Guides

Contents

Ramble Preamble

Unless you have a leaning towards mathematics, the chances are you will not have heard of Felix Hausdorff, nor his dimension. To condense the entire workings deserving of a research fellowship into a single word, Hausdorff Dimension is a mathematical calculation of *wiggliness*; the United Kingdom has one of the wiggliest coastlines of any country in the world and, as a result of being battered for millennia by great waves coming in from the Atlantic, the west coast is significantly wigglier than the east. Great for surfing it may be, but with the coast path stretching out to every windswept headland, winding its way in and around every sandy cove and wiggling its way down from clifftop to combe and, more often than not, immediately returning to lofty heights, the path is not for the faint hearted or flip-flop wearer.

According to the official South West Coast Path website, the total climb for the 630-mile National Trail is 35,031 metres, only 361 metres short of scaling Mount Everest four times. And, in compliance with the laws of gravity and coast path walking, what goes up must come down, so you need some good calf muscles, if nothing else.

Further figures tell us that the coast path passes through five Areas of Outstanding Natural Beauty, two World Heritage Sites, several Nature Reserves, a UNESCO Designated Biosphere Reserve and a National Park, and has around 4,000 signposts or waymarks, 921 stiles, 230 bridges and over 3,000 steps. That is, steps as you would find in a staircase. Walking the entire Path could easily equate to around 1.3 million footsteps.

But don't let me put you off; much like the onset of old age, it's a gradual thing; it does not happen overnight. In fact, averaging eleven miles a day (which even on the toughest of days usually gets you to your chosen end point in time for afternoon tea or a refreshing alcoholic beverage), the entire path takes around eight weeks to complete, with most walkers undertaking the path in weekly sections spread over several years.

Often on the South West Coast Path's social media page, people ask for tips and advice on walking the entire path over a single summer month. My advice is: DON'T, IT'S NOT A RACE. To repeat a quote often mis-attributed to the American philosopher, Ralph Waldo Emerson, "It's not the destination, it's the journey". Mind you, Emerson also said "Do not follow where the path may lead. Go instead where there is no path and leave a trail", which is not good advice when walking along the top of a cliff in foggy weather.

The South West Coast Path is repeatedly described as one of the world's greatest walks. Do you really want to set off each day before the sun has barely risen, come rain or shine, to rush past every welcoming teashop and every picturesque view whilst ignoring the amazing geology and often rare flora and fauna? Is there true satisfaction to be gained by walking at a brisk pace for twelve hours, only to arrive at your pre-booked accommodation as the sun's shadows draw long?

Take time to stop and watch peregrine falcons as they hover above the cliffs before swooping on their prey…

…sit and admire the seals and the dolphins; lookout off the headlands of Devon and Cornwall for basking sharks; plan a daytrip to Lundy Island, a Marine Conservation Zone where fishing is banned and puffins, razorbills, and guillemots thrive;

browse the Pannier Markets of Barnstaple and Bideford; poke your head into one of the many local museums; walk through the dunes at Braunton Burrows; make time to visit St Nicholas' Chapel and the Tunnels Beaches in Ilfracombe or King Arthur's Castle at Tintagel; cross the causeway to explore St Michael's Mount, climb Portland Bill lighthouse; or ride the sea tractor to Burgh Island.

Descend the disused tin mine at Geevor Heritage Centre; sit and look out to sea from Hawker's Hut, set into the cliffs at Morwenstow; pose for a cheesy photo next to the JOHN O'GROATS 874 fingerpost at Land's

End; admire feral goats clinging to the rockfaces in the Valley of Rocks; climb a Wreck Post; divert down a path to one of the secluded coves and explore the hidden caves; or, just sit, relax and look out to sea from the garden of a centuries-old village pub. These places need your custom to survive!

To repeat another quote, this time by either Ernest Hemingway or Ursula K. Le Guin (opinion is divided), "It's good to have an end to journey toward; but it is the journey that matters, in the end".

Before setting off, I must mention that the early stages of the coast path, from Minehead, through Exmoor National Park and along the north Devon coast to Lynmouth, are characterised by woodland paths, often edged with long grass. Ticks, by unhappy coincidence, enjoy wooded areas and long grass.

Although by no means all of them, some ticks carry the bacteria that causes Lyme disease. The most common symptom of Lyme disease is a large circular rash around a tick bite, often resembling the bullseye on a dartboard. The rash usually appears within two weeks of being bitten but can appear up to three months later and last for several weeks. Other tick-bite sufferers experience flu-like symptoms. Left untreated, the long-term symptoms of Lyme disease are very unpleasant.

Ticks are small, spider-like parasitic creatures which survive by gorging on blood. They don't jump; they don't fly; but what they do do is attach themselves to your exposed skin as you brush past them. If undetected, they will feed on your blood for several days until contentedly bloated. As refreshing as it is to be wearing a short-sleeved T-shirt and shorts on a warm summer's day, you may wish to consider long sleeves and trousers tucked into your socks. Also spray your clothes and exposed skin with an insect spray that contains DEET.

As a tick bite is not always painful, you may not notice it, so after a day of walking, check your skin for undesirable hangers on. To remove a tick safely, you will need either a tick-removal tool or a fine pair of tweezers. Grab the tick close to the skin and pull it off slowly, taking care not to crush it, then clean the bite with antiseptic.

Somerset

Give or take the odd kissing gate, the first 14 miles of the South West Coast Path is in Somerset, and before you leave it behind on Day 2 of the walk, it would be remiss of me to not tell you a little about this county. If you are covered in DEET and itching to get going, feel free to skip this chapter.

Somersetshire, to give the county its full name, has 11,500 listed buildings, 523 ancient monuments and 36 English Heritage sites, whilst the City of Bath, celebrated for its Roman Baths and Georgian architecture, is a UNESCO World Heritage Site. Pulteney Bridge in Bath is one of only four Palladian bridges left in the world. The bridge provided the backdrop for the scene of Inspector Javert's dramatic suicide in the 2012 musical drama *Les Miserables*.

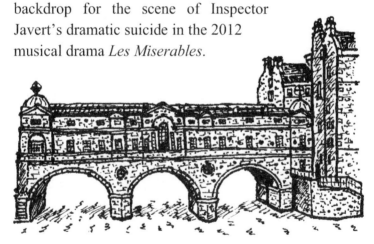

Whether Bath is included within the borders of Somerset is a brief question with a protracted answer.

To quote the title of a romantic comedy, it's complicated. In brief, there is a difference between England's administrative, geographic and historic county boundaries. Somerset's administrative boundary comprises of five districts, including *South Somerset* and *West Somerset*, the geographic boundary covers the entire administrative county plus the unitary authorities of *Bath and North East Somerset* and *North Somerset*, whilst the historic boundary covers the entire geographic boundary plus parts of the city of Bristol, south of the River Avon.

Covering 1,610 square miles (give or take a boundary or two) Somerset is the 7th largest county in England by area but, with a population recorded in the 2011 census of 908,554, only the 22nd largest by population. So, if you are not a local and you fancy moving to the county, there is plenty of room.

There is certainly plenty of room in the Quantock Hills, 38 square miles of heather and gorse heathland, oak woodland, flower-rich bogs and rugged coastline rising to Will's Neck, at 384 metres one of the highest points in Somerset.

South of Will's Neck, Fyne Court in the village of Broomfield was the home of electrical pioneer Andrew Crosse, who lived there from his birth in 1784. Aside from experimenting with electrocrystallization, research into discovering the polarity of the atmosphere under different weather conditions led to Crosse constructing a 1.25-mile-long insulated wire suspended from poles and trees. One of the first to develop large voltaic piles, he built a battery capable of releasing an electrical charge with accompanying sound loud enough to wake the dead, earning him the nickname "the thunder and lightning man".

Following one complex electrocrystallization experiment Crosse reported to his friends of finding a small insect, with several more appearing over the following days. Soon, several had become hundreds. A local newspaper learned of the incident and news spread through the country like a virulent rash, with enthusiastic reporters embellishing the story to give the impression that the mad scientist had "created" insects. With Crosse believed to have taken God's place as the creator of life, angry letters flooded in.

Although later analysis concluded that Crosse's instruments may have been contaminated by either cheese or dust mites (that's cheese mites, not cheese, and mites are arthropods, not insects) the modern internet of disinformation now claims that Crosse's life-giving experiments gave inspiration for author Mary Shelley's Gothic novel, *Frankenstein*. Given that Frankenstein was published in 1818 and Crosse's cheese-mite-contaminated experiments were in 1836, it is just as likely that the not-so-mad scientist had resolved the conundrum of time travel. Although in fairness the story may have legs, as Mary Shelley is thought to have known Crosse through a mutual friend, and she and her poet husband Percy reportedly attended a lecture by Crosse in London in December 1814. Furthermore, the Taunton Courier of Autumn 1836 reports (and I can't say for certain as my copy has recently gone out with the recycling) of Mary and Percy Shelley visiting Crosse at Fyne Court. Given that Percy Shelley drowned in a storm off the coast of Italy in 1822, time travel is looking increasingly plausible.

What is known for sure is that Crosse enjoyed pleasurable pursuits outside of his laboratory, as he sired seven children with his first wife and, following her passing, married a 23-year-old at the age of 66 and sired a further three children before dying of a stroke in July 1855.

Although Fyne Court was largely destroyed by a fire in 1894, you can still visit the National Trust owned garden and estate.

In addition to the Quantocks, there are three further Areas of Outstanding Natural Beauty in Somerset: the Blackdown Hills, the Mendips and much of Cranbourne

Chase. The Mendip Hills are mostly formed from Carboniferous limestone, and water erosion of the soft rock has peppered the upland with elaborate cave systems, not least the show cave of Wookey Hole, once owned by Madame Tussauds and, at the time of writing, former circus owner, Gerry Cottle; hence the reason for a penny arcade and other dubious money-spinning attractions.

Over 9,000 years old, *Cheddar Man*, Britain's oldest complete skeleton, was found in Gough's Cave. Cheddar Yeo, the largest underground river system in Britain, flows through Gough's Cave before emerging into Cheddar Gorge and flowing down through the village of Cheddar. Up to 137 metres in depth, Cheddar Gorge is one of the UK's greatest natural wonders.

On the southern edge of the Mendips is the cathedral city of Wells. The clock inside Wells Cathedral is a strong contender for the second oldest clock in the world; or, at least, the second oldest clockface, as the original mechanism, dated to between 1386 and 1392, now resides in the Science Museum in London. With a new mechanism installed in the 19th century, the astronomical clock follows the passing of the moon in its 30-day cycle.

Above the clock, jousting knights on horseback take to battle as the Quarter Jack strikes a bell with a hammer and two further bells with his heels to mark every quarter hour.

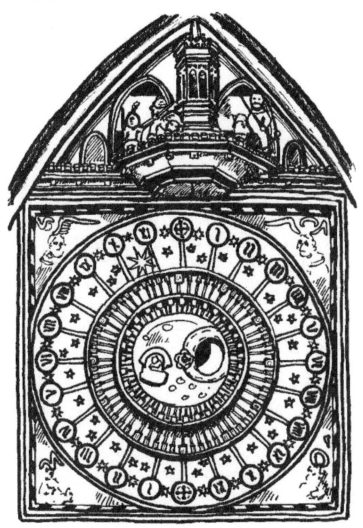

Wells is a popular filming location, often seen in the BBC adaptation of *Poldark* and again in the 2007 crime comedy *Hot Fuzz*. With a population of just 12,000, Wells is England's smallest city.

Over five times bigger and not a city, Taunton is the county town of Somerset. In 1886, Taunton became the first town in England to have electric street lighting permanently installed.

North of the Mendips and south to the Blackdown Hills are the lowlands of the Somerset Levels, 250 square miles of peaty moorland and coastal plain wetland, much of it below the level of spring high tide. The Celts and Saxons dubbed Somerset *The Land of the Summer*, as they could only live off the land during the summer because the area was prone to winter floods.

Before draining of the peatbogs, much of the Levels was little more than swampy marshland with isolated clumps of land. One such clump was the Isle of Althelney. Linked only by a protected causeway to East Lyng, King Alfred the Great used Althelney as a place of refuge before defeating the Viking army at the Battle of Edington in May 878. It was whilst on the Isle of Althelney that King Alfred famously let cakes that were baking burn. He was, at the time, watching over them for the wife of a pig farmer.

Aside from arable and dairy farming, the coastal wetlands sustain the UK's only commercially grown willow, used for, amongst many things, hot-air balloon passenger baskets and, increasingly, willow coffins. To celebrate the importance of willow to the Levels, a 40-foot-tall man woven from local willow over a metal frame stands in a field near the M5 at Bridgwater. Designed by artist Serena de la Hey, the *Willow Man* is affectionately known locally as the *Angel of the South*.

If you study a detailed map of the Somerset Levels and follow the lines of roads, tracks and the River Parrett, before your eyes will appear the *Girt Dog of Langport*.

Across the road from Walkeys Farm, the great hound's nose is at Burrow Mump, its ear at Earlake Moor and its tail at Wagg Drove. As names go, they are a copyrighter's dream.

Five miles from nose to tail, "the biggest dog in Britain" is said to defend the nearby town of Langport from Viking invasion.

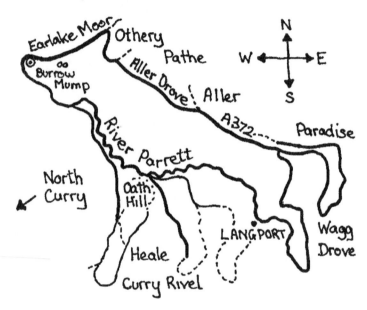

The earliest reference to the Girt Dog appears to be in 1895, in a verse recited during the local custom of wassailing. Its chorus begins:

The Girt Dog of Langport has burnt his long tail
And this is the night we go singing Wassail...

Wassailing is the custom of singing to trees in apple orchards to scare away evil spirits and encourage a good harvest for the following autumn. Originating as an Anglo-Saxon pagan ritual, the wassail should be celebrated on the evening of 05 January, the Twelfth Night, although it is more popularly celebrated 12 days later on 17 January, *Old Twelvy Night*, the correct date before the introduction of the Gregorian calendar in 1752.

The evening begins with the drinking of wassail punch, a hot mulled cider, a popular recipe being lambswool, made from traditional ale, sugar and baked apples and spices, topped with slices of toast. As the evening progresses, the Wassail Queen, wearing a crown festooned with ivy, lichen and mistletoe, leads a procession to the nearest orchard, where she is lifted into the branches of the biggest apple tree. Whilst villagers form a circle around the tree and pour wassail cider on its roots, the Wassail Princess passes the Queen some cider-soaked toast, which she dutifully ties amongst the branches as a gift to the tree spirits.

The Queen then recites a verse, following which the assembled crowd sing, shout, bang pots and pans and make as much noise as possible, until several farmers fire their rifles through the branches of the tree. If still alive, the Wassail Queen is lowered down and the semi-drunken rabble move on to the next orchard.

Sounding like a meal found on a gastropub specials board, *Ashen Faggot* is another popular custom, practised on Christmas Eve in both Somerset and Devon. A bundle of sticks, twigs or branches from an ash tree are bound with nine flexible ash strips, known as withies. With a fire lit using the remains of the previous year's faggots, the new "ashen faggots" are thrown to the flames. As the fire takes hold and each withy splits apart, onlookers celebrate with a drink, most commonly cider. According to tradition, unmarried women must each pick a faggot, with a belief that the first one whose withy splits will be the next to marry.

Punkie Night is a popular West Country custom celebrated in the Somerset village of Hinton St George on the last Thursday in October. Led by the Punkie King and Queen and accompanied by Morris dancers, children parade around the village carrying jack o'lanterns, whilst singing...

Punkie Night tonight
Punkie Night tonight
Adam and Eve wouldn't believe
It's Punkie Night tonight

The origins of the custom are murky, one suggestion being that the wives of the village may have made the original lanterns to search for their drunk husbands, lost on their way home from Chiselborough Fair.

A jack o'lantern, should you wish to be enlightened, is a hollowed-out pumpkin, mangelwurzel or other root vegetable, with a lit candle inside. The name is associated with *will-o-the-wisp*, an atmospheric ghost light that, in folklore, hovers at night over swamps and marshland, luring travellers to a sticky end. It is thought that the lights could be the wandering spirits of the dead or the work of the Devil; hence, their association with Halloween.

There are over 400 villages and hamlets in Somerset and the following deserve a mention for their names alone: Beardly Batch, Charlton Mackrell, Chedzoy, Clapton in Gordano, Compton Pauncefoot, Curry Mallet, Huish Episcopi, Nempnett Thrubwell, Preston Plucknett and Vobster.

In 1577, Thomas Coryat was born in the village of Odcombe. As a travel writer, Coryat is credited with introducing the table fork to England and the word *umbrella* to the English language.

Designing the first flushing toilet in 1596, poet and author Sir John Harington installed his new lavatorial invention in his manor house in the village of Kelston. He called his invention Ajax, *jakes* at the time being a slang word for toilet, and it was from this that the once-popular cleaning product took its name. Sir John is a strong contender for the origin of the expression *going to the John*. Harington being the godson of Queen Elizabeth I, the queen most likely used the toilet whilst on a visit; leading, it could be said, to the first royal flush.

In 1763, Reverend Augustus Toplady, preacher in the Mendips village of Blagden, was travelling through Burrington Combe when he was caught in a thunderstorm. Whilst sheltering under a rock, the story goes that he was inspired to compose the popular hymn *Rock of Ages*. The rock is now marked with a commemorative plaque.

Somerset boasts several musical locations and connections. The entire band of Portishead were born near Bristol, in the coastal town of Portishead. John Mellor, otherwise known as Joe Strummer, co-founder and lead singer of rock band The Clash, lived and died in the village of Broomfield. Famed clarinettist Acker Bilk was born in the village of Pensford and is buried a short walk away in All Saints churchyard in Publow. Born Bernard Stanley Bilk, he gained the nickname Acker from the Somerset slang for mate or friend. The scrumpy and western band The Wurzels topped the charts in 1976 with *The Combine Harvester* and had a further Top 10 hit with *I am a Cider Drinker*.

Of course, if you enjoy music festivals, there is a popular annual event at Glastonbury. Digressing somewhat, the town is also renowned for the *Glastonbury Holy Thorn*, and this is where I steal a passage from my earlier publication, *The Completely Useless Guide to Christmas*: According to legend, following the death of Jesus his great-uncle Joseph of Arimathea travelled to Britain, bringing with him the Holy Grail. Intending to spread the message of Christianity, Joseph travelled to the West Country, to the town of Glastonbury, where, pushing his walking stick into the ground beside him, he lay down to sleep. Upon awakening, he found the stick had both taken root and begun to flower. Joseph left his walking stick in the ground and, from that day, the Glastonbury thorn, unlike the more common, single-flowering hawthorn tree, magically blossomed every winter and spring.

During the English Civil War of 1642-51, the original tree that grew from the walking stick of Joseph of Arimathea was cut down and destroyed by Roundhead soldiers faithful to Oliver Cromwell, but not before secret cuttings were planted to cultivate further trees. Two surviving Glastonbury Holy Thorns grow in the grounds of the Church of St John the Baptist. From one of these "sacred thorns" a flowering sprig is sent every Christmas to the British monarch, a tradition dating back to the early 17th century.

Stealing, this time, from another of my earlier non-best sellers, *The Completely Useless Guide to England*...

On the coast of north Somerset, Birnbeck Pier links the seaside resort of Weston-super-Mare to a rocky outcrop, submerged at high tide, known as Birnbeck Island. During the Second World War, the Admiralty requisitioned the pier and bestowed it with the seaworthy title, *HMS Birnbeck*. HMS Birnbeck became the headquarters of the Inspectorate of Anti-Aircraft Weapons and Devices, commonly known, by the corruption of *weapons and devices*, as the *Wheezers and Dodgers*. Later to become the Directorate of Miscellaneous Weapons Development, the Wheezers and Dodgers conducted research into the development of unconventional weapons.

With famed scientist and engineer Barnes Wallis amongst their staff, unconventional successes included early development work on the "Bouncing Bomb".

Aside from Birnbeck Pier, Weston-super-Mare has a grander pier, aptly named the Grand Pier. Anthony Hopkins and Emma Thompson spend time on the pier in the 1993 film *The Remains of the Day*. The pier was rebuilt following a devastating fire in 2008.

To avoid being the butt of cheese-related humour, before joining the army in 1915, Reginald Cheese changed his surname to Cleese. On 27 October 1939, Reginald's son, John Cleese, was born in Weston-super-Mare. Children's author Roald Dahl referred to Weston-super-Mare in his autobiography as *Weston-super-Mud*, describing the town as a "slightly seedy seaside resort". For four years from the age of nine, Dahl attended St Peter's boarding school in the town. Although the school, which Dahl went on to describe as resembling "a private lunatic asylum", was demolished in the 1970s to make way for a housing estate, Weston-super-Mare's town council has since erected a blue plaque marking the spot in Dahl's honour, claiming that the author's schoolboy memories, as bad as they were, allowed him to develop a spirit for the style of dark humour that ultimately led to him writing wonderful children's books.

Somerset's literary heritage extends much further than Roald Dahl. Jane Austen, resident of Bath from 1801 to 1806, set both *Northanger Abbey* and *Persuasion* in the city. Evelyn Waugh lived and expired in the village of Combe Florey and is buried in a private plot of land next to St Peter and St Paul's churchyard, whilst poet T. S. Eliot's ashes are in St Michael and All Angels' Church in East Coker.

In 1912, Virginia Woolf and husband Leonard spent their honeymoon in the Plough Inn in Holford. The following year, with Virginia proscribed a hearty dose of country air following a recurring bout of mental illness, the couple returned to the 16th-century inn, Leonard writing in his autobiography of enjoying the Somersetshire breakfast.

Before you check in for the night in anticipation of a hearty Somersetshire breakfast, it would be remiss of me not to make mention of a ghostly tale... one night around the year 1555 a Spanish merchant arrived at the Plough Inn and struck up conversation with a group of locals. The locals, convinced that the well-attired and portly traveller was not short of a gold coin or two, plied him with alcohol and waited for him to retire to his room, whereupon they snuck upstairs and strangled him in his bed. The locals searched the room but found no coins, and that the ghost of the Spanish merchant returns to the inn from time to time to check that his gold remains safely hidden. His footsteps are said to be heard where the staircase to his room was located before being removed to make way for an extension, and a cloaked figure has been seen in an upstairs room of the pub.

For those not averse to a rhyming couplet, the Quantocks and the wooded slopes around Minehead are believed to be the location of the Hermit's home in *The Rime of the Ancient Mariner*, by Romantic poet Samuel Taylor Coleridge. Coleridge lived in the village of Nether Stowey, three miles south-west of Holford, and together with friend, fellow poet and (for a brief period) nearby Somerset resident William Wordsworth, would often wander the coast path and hills of an evening. At a time when Britain was at war with France, local gossip mongering apparently led to a government officer being dispatched from London to investigate the pair as French spies, the officer concluding that they were "mere poets".

Mere poets they may have been, but fans of long-distance poetry can now walk the 51-mile Coleridge Way from Nether Stowey, across the Quantock Hills and Exmoor, to Lynmouth. The path is appropriately waymarked with Quill signs.

Which conveniently brings me back to the subject of this book…

Day 1
Minehead to Porlock Weir

Distance: 8.9 miles
Ascent: 556 metres

So, Minehead, the start of the South West Coast Path; birthplace of science fiction writer Arthur C. Clarke and reputedly where Cecil Alexander wrote the popular hymn, *All Things Bright and Beautiful*. The hymn's lyrics *The purple headed mountain, the river running by* may refer to Grabbist Hill, overlooking the town, and the River Avill, which flows to the sea through nearby Snowdrop Valley.

If you are planning to travel to the start by public transport, what better way to arrive than on a steam train, curtesy of the *West Somerset Railway*. Opened in 1874, England's longest and one of the country's most scenic heritage railway lines passes over the Quantock Hills, with views across the Bristol Channel to south Wales.

Ahead of you as you leave the train is North Hill, the *head* of Mine*head* and the first of the coast path's many inclines. Visible on the lower slope of North Hill is St Michael's Church, which offers views of the town and harbour. The tower of St Michael's used to display a beacon light to guide ships into the harbour, whilst the hours of the clock were struck by a carved wooden character dressed in a green jacket, breeches and an apparent Santa hat. Known as *Jack Hammer*, he currently stands on the top right of the church's 15th-century vaulted rood screen, holding a bell. The bell is rung manually on Sundays to announce the start of the morning service.

A popular time to begin walking the South West Coast Path is late April or early May, as daylight hours increase, the weather is hopefully warmer and the beachside bars and cafes en route open for the summer season.

Arrive at this time and you may well witness *Minehead Hobby Horse*, a four-day festival beginning on the eve of May Day. The festival involves large boat-shaped hobbyhorses decorated with brightly coloured ribbons, with domed heads and painted tin faces. Accompanied by drummers and accordionists, there is much dancing and, in a finale known as *Bootie Night*, a "victim" kicked ten times whilst being held down by one of the hobbyhorses.

The festival may have begun as a way of deterring Viking invaders or, equally plausible, following the arrival in Minehead of a ghostly ship devoid of captain or crew.

The captain and crew could well have been found in *The Mermaid*, a one-time ship chandler's and later an inn, home to *Old Mother Leakey*, Minehead's famous whistling ghost, who purportedly whistled up a storm every time one of her son Alexander's ships attempted to dock in the harbour. Before gaining notoriety as a whistling ghost, *Old Mother* Susanna Leakey lived in The Mermaid and, upon her death, was buried in St Michael's Church on 5 November 1634. Unfortunately, her grave is nowhere to be found, unlike The Mermaid, which is now *Tea at the Quay*, a welcoming refreshment stop located, as the name suggests, on The Quay. Although no longer famous for its ghost, if you listen carefully you may just hear a whistling kettle.

And so, suitably refreshed, a scone's throw from Tea on the Quay brings you to the public art marking the official start of the South West Coast Path.

Designed by art student Sarah Ward and sculpted by Owen Cunningham, the almost four-metre-high galvanized steel sculpture depicts two hands holding a paper map of the coast, the grid above the coastline left open so that the sea and sky are visible behind.

As one not given to effuse about such things, I consider this a wonderful piece of public art, most worthy to mark the start of what has often been voted one of the best long-distance walks in the world.

Following a gentle start, the coast path leaves Minehead harbour and heads up, and then along, Greenaleigh Lower Road, before an acorn sign and arrow indicates that the path to the left doubles back uphill via a set of steps. Miss this and continue along the road through Greenaleigh Farm and you will find yourself amongst the ruins of Burgundy Chapel. Do not despair, to the left of the chapel a narrow stony path takes you up Burgundy Chapel Combe, where you can re-join the coast path. The path is quite steep, but there is a welcome bench at the top. You may wish to sit and study your map.

If you didn't miss the previously mentioned sign, the coast path climbs steeply into Moor Wood. During the Second World War the wood was used by US and Canadian tank troops for training exercises, and the ramps used for unloading the vehicles are still in place. If you come across what looks like a set of dragon's teeth, they were set into the hillside to stop the tanks sliding into the sea. You might also spot a radar hut, along with several cobble-clad pillboxes close to the shoreline.

You are now entering the Holnicote Estate, which covers over 5,000 hectares of Exmoor National Park.

To preserve the family pile from future development, in 1917 Sir Thomas Dyke Acland, 12th Baronet, loaned Holnicote House and estate, which he described as "one of the most beautiful pieces of wild country to be found in England", to the National Trust on a 500-year lease. With the lease imminently due to expire in 2417, in 1944 Sir Richard Thomas Dyke Acland, 15th Baronet, gifted the house and estate outright, throwing in Killerton, an 18th-century stately home in the village of Broadclyst, north east of Exeter, for good measure.

After passing the bench above Burgundy Chapel, the path soon divides, with the option of an upland route via Selworthy Beacon and Bossington Hill, or, adding half a mile and potentially an hour to the day's walk, a rugged but scenic route that hugs the side of the hill.

At 308 metres, Selworthy Beacon is one of Somerset's three peaks, and the site of the remains of Bury Castle Iron Age hill fort. A little way inland from Selworthy Beacon are Katherine's Well and Agnes Fountain, both thought to have been named after daughters in the Acland family, along with a Wind and Weather hut, built by the family as a memorial to Sir Thomas, the 10th Baronet, a great lover of walking who would visit the Beacon every Sunday, regardless of the weather.

The paths meet again just before Hurlstone Point, where there is a disused coastguard lookout shelter. Around 3.5 miles south-west of Hurlstone Point, at the top of Porlock Hill, are two thick sandstone slabs known as the *Whit Stones*. Were they not resting in a reclining position amongst the heather and daffodils, the stones would both stand around 1.5 metres tall. Once referred to as the *White Stones*, the name change aptly reflects their current liberal coating of lichen and bird poo.

According to legend, the Devil aided by an unnamed giant threw the Whit Stones from Hurlstone Point, hence the point's name. Alternatively, they may well be either boundary markers or part of a stone circle or burial chamber.

Hurlstone Point looks down to Porlock Bay and across to Porlock Weir, with Foreland Point in the distance.

One mile south, the path takes you to the hamlet of Bossington, where you can enjoy a welcome break at Kitnors Tea Room, a 15th-century Grade II listed cottage with a garden.

From Bossington, the coast path used to run along the shingle ridge across Porlock Bay. In 1996, waves breached the ridge in a storm and the fields inland now flood with each high tide, creating a nationally important nature reserve and saltmarsh. The path now follows the high tide mark around the edge of the marsh.

On 29 October 1942, a US Air Force Liberator plane was returning from a routine U-boat patrol mission over the Bay of Biscay. In poor weather conditions, the plane clipped the top of Bossington Hill and crashed into the marsh of Porlock Bay. Of the twelve crewmembers onboard, only one survived: Staff Sergeant H. E. Thorpe. As you cross the bay you will pass a memorial and plaque listing the names of the lost crew.

The path around the bay emerges onto the shingle of Porlock beach, where at low tide the remains of a submerged forest can be seen, the area being several miles inland until sea levels rose in the Bristol Channel about 7,000 years ago.

Before this point, if there is still time in the day you may wish to divert down one of the many paths that lead you into Porlock village. Personally, I think it would be rude not to, and you can always return via the same route or re-join the coast path a little further on.

At the odd times that there is an exceptional high tide, the new path across the bay may also flood, so you will have no choice but to divert inland. If so, from Porlock follow the signposted toll road past the village hall.

The toll road bypasses Porlock Hill, which is renowned for its 1-in-4 gradient, the steepest incline on an A-road in Britain. I remember as a knobbly-kneed youngster in short trousers (the knees and lack of fashion sense continue to this day, much to the dismay of the fashion police) my parents taking me on holiday to Porlock, and our attempt to drive up the hill in the first family car, a Hillman Husky. After much gear grinding and little upward progress, it was decided that greater pleasure would be gained in taking the alternative and more scenic toll road.

Immediately past the village hall, turn right onto a footpath. The footpath takes you to Porlock Weir, the end of today's walk, around 1.5 miles west of the village.

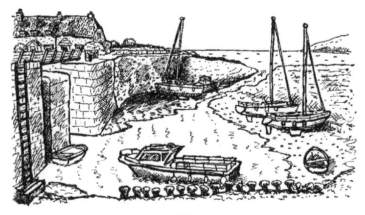

The name of Porlock derives from the Old English *Portloc*, or *Portloca*, a port location, Porlock Weir being the village's harbour. For more information on the village and weir, the one-room *Boat Shed Museum* is worth a visit; admission free and donations to support the local lifeboat.

There are two Ship Inns in Porlock, the "Top" Ship in the village, and the "Bottom" Ship in the Weir. In August 1799, Romantic poet Robert Southey stayed in the Top Ship.

In a letter to his brother he remarked that his room had a decent chamber pot and no fleas. The following day, in a nook by the inn fire, Southey composed his sonnet *To Porlock*. The nook is now known as Southey Corner.

Built in 1290, The Ship is one of the oldest inns in the country.

Also dating to the 13th century, the Church of St Dubricius in Porlock is dedicated to the saint who crowned King Arthur.

Since a lightning strike in 1703, the church has been missing the top of its slate spire.

Aside from being a village, the Collins English Dictionary lists porlock as a verb, meaning *to interrupt or intrude at an awkward moment*. The verb originates from Samuel Taylor Coleridge, who claimed that he composed *Kubla Khan*, one of his most famous poems, in 1797 during an opium-induced dream. Awoken from the dream by an unexpected visitor from Porlock, Coleridge promptly forgot all but ten of the lines. Eventually published in 1816, the final poem was reduced from a dreamy 200-plus lines to just 54.

Exmoor

With its towering cliffs, rocky headlands, grand waterfalls and a wealth of caves and natural beauty, in 1991 Exmoor's coast deservedly received Heritage status.

Named after the River Exe, Exmoor includes the Brendon Hills, the East Lyn Valley and the Vale of Porlock. Much of it is purple heather and yellow gorse-covered moorland, with a splattering of villages and hamlets, rising to Dunkery Beacon, 519 metres above sea level. Parts of it are ancient woodland, the seven miles of coast between Porlock and Foreland Point being the  longest continual stretch of coastal woodland in England. At a shade over 60 metres when measured in 2009, a Douglas fir at Nutcombe Bottom, near the village of Dunster, is officially the tallest tree in England. Planted in 1876, the trunk of the lofty fir is estimated to weigh 50 tonnes.

Once a Royal Forest and hunting ground, Exmoor gained National Park status in 1954. The park covers an area of 267.5 square miles, 71% of which is in Somerset and 29% in Devon, its northern boundary marked by 34 miles of the Bristol Channel coast. I am not 100% up to date with UK National Measurement and Regulation Office guidelines on slope measurement but, were a cliff to be defined as having a vertical incline of greater than 60%, the Exmoor stretch of coast boasts the highest sea cliffs on mainland Britain.

Great Hangman, just east of Combe Martin, is the highest point on the South West Coast Path, rising to 318 metres above sea level, with a cliff face dropping 244 metres. To put this in perspective, the famed white cliffs of Dover rise to 110 metres. A little further on, Great Hangman's sister cliff, *Little Hangman*, marks the western edge of Exmoor. The cliffs gain their names from the thick layer of Hangman Grits sandstone under foot. Or do they? With *hang* being the Saxon word for slope and *man* derived from *mynedd*, Celtic for hill (as in *The Old Man of Coniston* in the Lake District), the literal translation of hangman would be *sloping hill*. Then again, there is the story of a sheep rustler climbing the hill with a stolen ewe slung over his shoulder. Whilst he paused to rest, the sheep attempted to escape, and in the animal's struggles the cord binding its legs became twisted around the rustler's neck, hanging him.

Great Hangman features in *Meet the Tiger*, the first in a successful series of novels by Leslie Charteris featuring antihero detective Simon Templar, aka *The Saint*. Templar hides in an abandoned First World War pillbox on Great Hangman whilst investigating a Chicago gangster holed out in Combe Martin, referred to in the book as Baycombe.

In non-antihero literature, Exmoor will forever be associated with *Lorna Doone: A Romance of Exmoor*. Based on a true story, Richard Doddridge Blackmore's 1869 novel is set in the Doone Valley and surrounding area, with Lorna's wedding to John Ridd taking place in the 15th-century Church of St Mary in the village of Oare.

Blackmore reputedly wrote several of the chapters of Lorna Doone in the bar of the Royal Oak Inn in the nearby village of Withypool. The loft above the bar later served as a studio for famed artist, Alfred Munnings. Undercover research also exposes Maxwell

Knight, later to be a successful writer, radio broadcaster and M15 spymaster, who together with his wife Gwladys owned the Royal Oak in the 1930s. Covert rumour is that Ian Fleming partly based the character of *M*, James Bond's boss and Head of MI6, on the former publican. If that is not enough claims to fame, during World War II, whilst beaches in the West Country were being used as practise for the D-Day landings, General Dwight Eisenhower used a part of the pub as a base for operational planning.

A stone's throw south-east of Withypool, crossing the shallow waters of the River Barle, are the Tarr Steps, thought to be the longest and oldest clapper bridge in the UK.

At 55 metres, the longest it may be, but its age is less certain, dated between prehistoric and medieval. I would place my money on medieval, given that the name *clapper* is believed to have derived either from the Anglo-Saxon *cleaca*, meaning *bridging the steppingstones*, or the medieval Latin *claperius*, meaning *pile of stones*. And that sums it up, seventeen large slabs each weighing around two tonnes, sitting on piles of stones, designated by English Heritage as a Grade I listed structure and Scheduled Ancient Monument due to its architectural and historical significance.

But, could English Heritage be wrong?! Local legend once again intervenes, the slabs apparently put in place by the Devil; the Devil would not allow anyone to use his bridge and witnesses later observed a black cat walking across, only to vanish midway in a cloud of smoke. Following an altercation with the local vicar the Devil backed down, agreeing that any person could cross unharmed, providing he kept the right to sunbathe on the stones.

If you happen to have a set of binoculars in your backpack (or better still a telescope), with night-time darkness protected by strict measures to prevent light pollution, Exmoor is a world-renowned stargazing destination, one of only four International Dark Sky Reserves (and one Dark Sky Park) in the UK. Autumn sees the annual *Exmoor Dark Skies Festival*, with stargazey pie and non-light refreshments on offer.

☼ ☼ ☼

Considered one of the oldest breeds in the world, wild ponies have roamed free on Exmoor for at least 50,000 years. While the moor was used during the Second

World War as a training ground, their numbers dropped to only 50. Although numbers have since recovered, with only 390 breeding females, the ponies are classified as endangered by the Rare Breeds Survival Trust.

Exmoor is also home to a herd of red deer. Around 12 years old, 2.7 metres tall and weighing an estimated 136 kgs, Britain's largest known wild animal, a red deer dubbed the *Emperor of Exmoor*, was reported killed in the National Park during the rutting season in October 2010 by a licensed hunter. With no physical evidence found at the scene, the story of the Emperor's demise was dismissed as a tale concocted by an activist campaigning for a ban on the hunting of wild animals.

Speaking of wild animals, beware the *Beast of Exmoor*, a phantom cat which may live in old mine workings and can leap a six-foot fence with ease. Described as either black, dark grey or tan and measuring between four and eight feet from nose to tail, locals have likened the Beast (with its size-changing and chameleon abilities) to either a leopard, cougar, puma or panther. Phew, at least it is not a lion!

First reported in the 1970s, it is suggested that the cat could have been released from a private collection in the wake of the introduction of the Dangerous Animals Act in 1976, making it illegal for large exotic "pets" to be kept in captivity outside of zoos. With numerous rumours of further sightings, including one report of it being seen fishing in the River Barle, the Beast gained notoriety in 1983 when a farmer from South Molten claimed to have lost more than one hundred sheep over a three-month period, all with their throats torn. Following Ministry of Agriculture orders the Royal Marines sent snipers into the National Park. With no follow up information on their withdrawal, they may still be there.

After a photo claiming to be the Beast was published in the West Somerset Free Press in 1989, the Daily Express, taking a break from its usual severe weather warning cover stories, offered a reward for its capture or killing. The reward remains unclaimed.

From the Beast of Exmoor to a beast of burden, and the tale (or tail!) of *Zulu the Donkey*. At 310 metres above sea level, Stoke Pero Church is the highest church on Exmoor. Built in the 13th century, the church underwent extensive restoration at the end of the 20th century, with only the tower and porch remaining of the original structure. The timbers used in the rebuilding of the roof were said to have been hauled up from Porlock twice a day by a donkey by the name of Zulu, and the overworked animal is commemorated for its efforts in a portrait by local writer and artist, Hope Bourne, on display in the church.

Day 2
Porlock Weir to Lynmouth

Distance: 12.1 miles
Ascent: 962 metres

From Porlock Weir, the coast path passes behind the
pub and hotel, through a gate and inland of red-tiled
former stables, crossing a field to join Worthy Toll
Road, just before the arches of the Worthy Combe Toll
Lodge.

Leave the road, taking the right-hand archway gate to
the ruins of what was originally Ashley Combe House
and gardens.

Built in 1799, Ashley Combe House was owned by
Lord William King, later the 8th Baron King. On 8 July
1835, Lord King married the Honourable Augusta Ada

Byron, daughter of Lady Byron and her poet husband, Lord Byron. The couple spent their honeymoon at the house, which later became their summer retreat. In 1838, Lord King added Viscount Ockham and Earl of Lovelace to his flourishing list of titles, his wife in turn becoming both Countess of Lovelace and Lady Ada Lovelace.

With Ada bringing a considerable fortune to the marriage, the couple set about making substantial improvements to the house and grounds, adding decorative towers, turrets and an impressive clocktower, along with Italianate terraced walled gardens joined by a spiral staircase, and woodland walks with hidden archways and ornamental follies. Tunnels were constructed so that tradesmen and their carts could approach the house without being seen from

inside, with further tunnels and a staircase built by Swiss mountaineers to provide privacy for Ada when she descended to a bathhouse built into the cliff above her private beach.

Meanwhile, gardeners planted an arboretum of trees, including Lebanon and Bermuda cedars, with an estimated 100,000 trees transported from Lord King's Scottish estate.

Far more than a Lady of the Manor who relished her privacy, Ada Lovelace was a keen writer and mathematician and enjoyed many learned conversations on the terraces overlooking the elaborate gardens with her good friend, Charles Baggage. The two discussed Babbage's idea for a calculating machine, and between 1842 and 1843 she translated a publication catchily entitled *Sketch of the Analytical Engine Invented by Charles Babbage, Esq.,* written by Italian mathematician and mechanical engineer, Luigi Menabrea. Ada Lovelace's elaborate notes describing an algorithm designed to be implemented by a machine are today consider by many to be the world's first computer software program, with Babbage's machine the world's first mechanical computer.

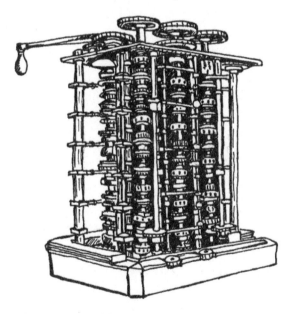

This point is arguable, with other historians lending their weight behind Babbage's earlier notes. I for one, at this point on the walk, am happy to sit on a fence (or crumbling garden wall).

Nonetheless, Ada Lovelace has since achieved worldwide recognition for the part she played in early computer development, with *Ada Lovelace Day*, an international celebration of the achievements of women in science, technology, engineering and maths, held annually on the second Tuesday in October. In 1979, the US Department of Defence named their new high-level computer programming language "Ada" in her honour, and the name continues in computer use to this day.

Sadly, Ada Lovelace died of cancer in 1852 aged only 36, and with her husband also long passed, during the Second World War Ashley Combe House found use as an orphanage run by Dr Barnardo's children's charity. Renamed Worthy Manor, in 1950 it briefly became a Country Club before closing and falling into disrepair, finally demolished in 1974 on safety grounds. The remains of the staircase to the beach and a small fireplace in the upper room of the bathhouse are still visible.

Leaving the estate, the coast path zigzags its way up the wooded hillside until opening out to a clearing where, nestled below in a quiet combe looking out to sea, sits St Beuno's Church, reputedly the smallest complete parish church in England. Seating 33 at a squash, the interior of the church measures just 10.7 by 3.6 metres.

Grade I listed, the main walls of the church are pre-Norman, dating to the 11th century, if not earlier, with various bits since added and replaced. Set into the sanctuary wall are two lights of an original window, carved from one block of sandstone. Above the exterior of the window is a smiling feline face.

Aside from a couple of houses, the St Bueno's Church is barely all that remains of the hamlet of Culbone. Inhabited on and off since 3,500 BC, with no track or road other than what is now the coast path, by the 13th century Culbone's remote location had made it a place for the banishment of undesirables. Amongst others, atheists, the mentally insane, French prisoners and witches were abandoned to fend for themselves. Nevertheless, it appears that church services continued as, according to Court records, in 1280 the chaplain of St Bueno's, a man by the name of Thomas, was charged with murdering Albert of Esshe with a hatchet blow to the head.

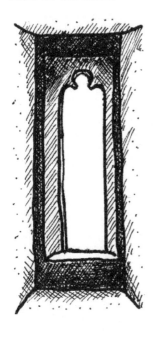

By the 16th century the not-so-fortunate witch community were finding themselves either drowned or burned at the stake, and, with a leper colony now living in the surrounding woods, a small window known commonly as a leper's squint was set into the north wall of the church so that the infected could peer in to watch services without sitting amongst the congregation.

Taking a few backwards steps to yesterday's walk, and (as mentioned) since being struck by lightning in 1703, the Church of St Dubricius in Porlock has been missing the top of its slate spire. According to local folklore, following the lightning strike the storm carried the spire all the way to Culbone, where it now rests atop St Bueno's.

After crossing the stream by the stone-arched bridge you have a choice of two routes, both around the same distance, the slightly shorter and official lower route passing through Culbone Wood and the not-so-official upper route, via Silcombe Farm, offering views across the Bristol Channel to the coast of Wales.

With moist coastal air, a damp microclimate and resultant thriving undergrowth, Culbone Wood has been described as Britain's temperate rainforest. Although mostly sessile oak, the woodland is home to seven species of rare whitebeam trees, three of the species found only on the north Devon and Exmoor coast.

Depending on the species, the under surface of the whitebeams' leaves may be coated with a distinctive silvery felt, the trees sporting showy white blossoms in the spring and either red, brown or orange berries in the autumn.

The Culbone Wood path and the not-so-official upper path meet below Sugarloaf Hill before wiggling around Yenworthy Combe and Steeple Sturt and crossing Coscombe Stream. The stream marks the county border; you are now in Devon. In a few paces the path opens to a forest track, part of the driveway heading to Glenthorne House.

Set in 77 acres of woodland, Glenthorne House was the vision of Reverend Walter Halliday, the eldest surviving son of Simon Halliday, a naval surgeon and banker from Scotland, who amassed a great fortune during the Napoleonic Wars. Upon his father's death in 1829, Halliday resigned from the church and, in keeping with the terms of his inheritance, set about finding the perfect location to build a country estate in the family name. Following in the footsteps of the Romantic poets he greatly admired, he travelled to the West Country and settled in nearby Countisbury, using his newly-acquired wealth to buy the entire 7,000-acre parish and establish himself as the local squire. Halliday then set to work on the plans for Glenthorne House, a grand Tudor Gothic manor house looking out to sea on what is said to be the only piece of flat land between Lynmouth and Porlock.

Flat it may be but before construction could start workers had to build a driveway to connect it to the main road. Zigzagging its way down the steep hillside, the driveway stretches for three miles, with a further path built down to the beach so that local pinkish stone and other building materials could arrive by sea. Work on the main part of the house was completed in 1831, with later extension works adding new kitchens, a billiard room, large conservatory and library wing.

With several outhouses also added, as you pass through the estate, keep your eyes peeled for the icehouse, an old trout pool and a coach house that looks like it would not be out of place in a gnome world.

When Walter Halliday died childless in 1872 at the age of 94, due to a quirk of inheritance law the family fortune returned to Scotland whilst the estate passed to his nephew, William. Allowed to draw on the fortune only for "capital improvements", William invested money in the *Lynton and Barnstaple Railway*, dying on 11 May 1898, the very day that the first train arrived in Lynton. The estate passed to William Halliday's son, Ben. In 1910, Ben Halliday was elected Liberal MP for Bridgewater, serving in David Lloyd-George's coalition government, where he championed Women's Suffrage, the passing of the *Representation of the People Act* in 1918 granting the all women over the age of thirty the right to vote for the first time in British history.

Head west on the driveway towards Glenthorne House until, at the brow of the hill, turn right down a set of wooden steps. The steps pass a small natural spring beneath a 19th-century stone cairn and cross.

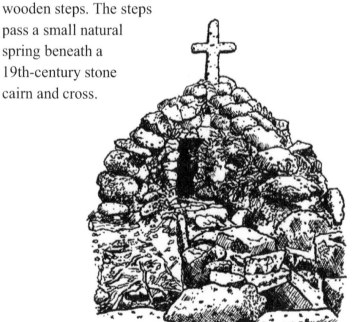

Intriguingly named *Sister's Fountain*, the spring water is said to have quenched the thirst of Joseph of Arimathea while en route to Glastonbury. His ancient journey, with feet walking upon England's mountains green, may have inspired the famed William Blake poem and later hymn, *Jerusalem*.

The path continues north, re-joining the driveway and passing between a pair of unimposing stone gate pillars topped by carved wild-boar heads, marking the official entrance to the estate.

To your left, the Glenthorne Pinetum was planted with exotic species of trees in the 1850s, including what is now a 50-metre giant redwood, one of the tallest trees in England.

Passing seaward of a woodland lodge, the path ahead, following the contours of the hillside, is especially beautiful in spring and early summer, with yellow gorse to the left, lilac rhododendrons to the right and the odd glimpse of the tree-clad headland of Desolation Point ahead. Below Desolation Point is the rocky outcrop of Sir Robert's Chair.

The path soon crosses the wonderfully named Pudleep Gurt, a gurt being local dialect for a gully.

At Foreland Point an access road leads north from the coast path to Lynmouth Foreland Lighthouse, worthy of a half-mile detour for views back along the coast.

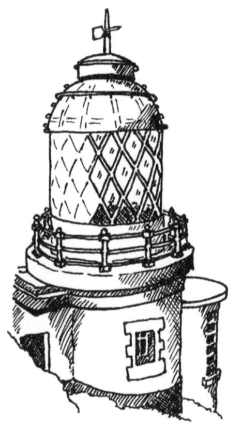

The headland marks the most northerly point of the coast path walk. Safest return to the path is by the access road, the alternative route south-west of the lighthouse not for the faint-hearted, especially in rough weather and fierce winds.

Continuing west to cross The Foreland, Lynton and Lynmouth come into view, Lynton connected to its lower neighbour by a funicular railway. The eagle-eyed may also get their first view of Sillery Sands, a secluded nudists beach just east of Lynmouth. At lower tides there may be more than a fair bit of sand exposed.

From The Foreland, the coast path makes a steady descent to the hamlet of Countisbury, where refreshments are on offer at the 13th-century Blue Ball Inn. The coaching inn's name dates to the late 18th century, when a blue ball attached to a pole outside would be raised to signal that a resident required transportation.

A further 1.5 miles takes you down to Lynmouth Harbour, the end of today's walk.

While you search for tick bites and early signs of blisters, take a moment to remember the one-time heroic feat of the crew of the Lynmouth lifeboat. On 12 January 1899, the 1,900-ton ship *Forrest Hall*, with 18 men onboard, was reported as floundering with a broken rudder in a severe gale off Porlock Weir. A telegraph arrived urgently requesting assistance from *Louisa*, the Lynmouth lifeboat. With the seas proving too turbulent for a launch, 18 horses and 100 men hauled the boat up the 1-in-4 gradient Countisbury Hill, stopping for refreshment and repair of a carriage wheel at the Blue Ball Inn. Twenty men, including the 14 crew, then hauled the lifeboat across Exmoor before dropping down Porlock Hill and into Porlock Weir. Launched into the weir's sheltered waters, the crew rowed for an hour in treacherous seas, rescuing the crew of the stricken Forrest Hall with no loss to life (aside from four of the horses, which died of exhaustion.) The celebrated journey took 11 hours.

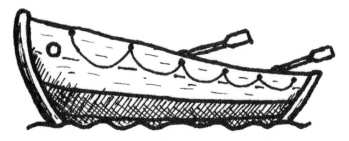

Lynmouth is squashed into the gorge of the West Lyn and East Lyn rivers, the waters meeting as they flow through the village. Flowing through the village resulted in disaster when, with a storm depositing 23 cm of rain within 24 hours on Exmoor, during the night of 15-16 August 1952, floodwaters poured down off the sodden moors, fallen trees and other debris forming a dam across the upper reaches of the West Lyn valley. The dam eventually gave way, the resultant huge wave descending on Lynmouth, taking 34 lives and washing away or seriously damaging around 100 buildings and 28 of the 31 river crossings. Whilst rebuilding the village, the rivers were widened and diverted away from the centre. The site where houses once stood on the bank of the East Lyn towards Watersmeet is now a memorial garden and a memorial hall dedicated to the disaster, with photos and a scale model of the village before the flood, is located opposite the harbour.

The stone folly on Lynmouth's quay is the Rhenish Tower, an exact replica of a tower built in 1860 for a General Rawdon to store saltwater for his invigorating baths. The original tower was washed away in the great flood. A beacon on the tower helps guide boats into the small harbour.

70

Honeymooning in Lynmouth with his wife Margaret in 1746, artist Thomas Gainsborough described the popular seaside village as "the most beautiful for the landscape painter this country can boast".

In 1799, poet Robert Southey wrote in his journal, "Even without the sea this would be one of the finest scenes I have ever beheld". He went on to remark upon Lynmouth's Alpine appearance, leading to the village becoming affectionately referred to as *England's Little Switzerland*. Fellow poet Percy Shelley expressed similar glowing views when, newly married, he holidayed in Lynmouth in 1812 with his first wife Harriet. It was during this time that he wrote *Queen Mab; A Philosophical Poem*.

Involved in radical politics, whilst in Ireland Shelley had written a political pamphlet about the French Revolution, decrying the rights of the Government. The pamphlet, entitled *A Declaration of Rights*, was considered too radical for British distribution, and whilst in Lynmouth Shelley was apparently seen in the waters of the harbour launching copies of the pamphlet hidden inside toy boats waterproofed with wax. He was also seen on the beach, attempting to set adrift copies sealed in boxes tied to handmade hot-air balloons. Reported by the Town Clerk of Barnstaple, Shelley only escaped prosecution as the pamphlets were unsigned.

The newly married couple stayed in Woodbine Villa, now Shelley's Cottage Hotel, a Georgian building on Watersmeet, just south of where the West

Lyn and East Lyn converge; or they may not have, the location of the couple's nine-week stay an ongoing argument. Shelley's Cottage Hotel claims to hold documentary proof, namely an article in the North Devon Herald dated 23 October 1901 celebrating the 100th birthday of a Miss Agnes Groves, who lived in Woodbine Villa at the time of the couple lodging there. Staking a counterclaim, the Rising Sun Hotel on the Harbourside, owners of nearby Shelley's Cottage, lists among items of proof that an ode written by Shelley was found in the one-bedroomed thatched cottage.

Don't you hate it when you check out and later discover you left an ode in the bedside cupboard?

Oh, Percy Shelley, where did you stay,
When you and your young bride went away?
Was it at the Woodbine Villa,
And what became of your flotilla?

With the Napoleonic Wars raging across Europe in the early part of the 19th century preventing foreign holidays, Lynmouth became increasingly popular as a holiday resort. Although difficult to reach across Exmoor, holidaymakers began to arrive on paddle steamers from south Wales, Bristol and other Channel ports. For Lynmouth to thrive it needed to expand and, squeezed into a gorge, the only way was up. Expand it did, into Lynton, perched over 150 metres up on the top of the cliff. All very well but reaching Lynton either involved a strenuous walk or meant the hiring of a donkey or in a horse drawn carriage ride up a steep hill. And with holidaymakers came the need to transport coal, foodstuffs and other essentials. Not surprisingly the horses had a short working life.

A solution emerged in 1881 with the proposal to build a water-powered funicular railway. With two carriages fixed to a single continuous cable, water would be pumped from the West Lyn up to a storage tank below the railway's upper carriage. The upper carriage would become heavier than the lower carriage, and like a set of weighing scales adhering to the laws of

73

gravity, once the brake was released the carriages would automatically change places. The water in the tank of the lower carriage would then be drained as the upper tank was being filled, and the process would continue.

Following lengthy planning and design work, construction eventually began in 1887, the railway opening in 1890. With the road proving too steep for early motorcars, the carriages – each designed to carry up to 40 passengers – were also used for transporting vehicles. Rising 152 metres with a 1-in-1.72 gradient, the Lynton & Lynmouth Cliff Railway is the world's highest and steepest water-powered funicular in operation.

Apart from the South West Coast Path, Lynmouth is on the route of the Tarka Trail, retracing the pawed steps of the fictional otter in Henry Williamson's 1927 novel, *Tarka the Otter*. The coastal village also marks the western end of the Coleridge Way from Nether Stowey, and the northern end of the Devon Coast-to-Coast walk (As well as two National Parks, Devon is of course the only English county to have two separate coastlines).

Devon

Devonshire, Shire of the Devonians, commonly known as Devon, is England's 4th largest county, covering an area of 2,590 square miles. With its population barely scraping 1.2 million, the county ranks 39th in density out of England's 48 Ceremonial counties; even more sparsely populated than neighbouring Somerset. What it lacks in population it makes up for in tarmac, the 8,000-mile network of motorways, roads and lanes being the longest of any county. If the Department for Transport straightened all the roads in Devon and placed them end-to-end, they would stretch from the UK to the Falkland Islands.

For driver safety I should just warn at this point of the B3212 between Two Bridges and Postbridge, a section of road of particular note for a pair of disembodied hairy hands, said to grab at the steering wheel or handlebars of moving vehicles and motorbikes, forcing the driver to career off the road. Following many reported sightings, in 1924 one of the hairy hands was seen attempting to gain access to a caravan. Investigations eventually determined that the accidents (aside from the caravan incident) were due to the adverse camber of the road's surface, which has since been uncambered.

The lack of people in Devon may be due in part to the 29 per cent of Exmoor National Park within its borders, along with 100 per cent of Dartmoor National

Park, an area of granite and peat bog moorland stretching for over 368 square miles, the largest open space in southern England.

While filming the 2012 adaptation of *War Horse*, director Steven Spielberg used several locations on Dartmoor, mostly around the villages of Meavy and Sheepstor. He is quoted as saying at the time, "I have never before, in my long and eclectic career, been gifted with such an abundance of natural beauty as I have experienced filming War Horse on Dartmoor … and, with two-and-a-half weeks of extensive coverage of landscapes and skies, I hardly scratched the surface of the visual opportunities that were offered to me."

※　※　※

At 621 metres above sea level, the highest point on Dartmoor is *High Willhays*, soaring a full two metres above its neighbour, *Yes Tor*. High Willhays and Yes Tor are the highest peaks in the south of England. Although not overly lofty, climbing Yes Tor when a red flag is flying from its peak is not advisable since it lies within a British Army firing range. One can, however, view a photo of it on the cover of the Yes album, *Tormato*, albeit with the tor obscured by splodges of tomato.

Balanced precariously upon a small pivotal stone on Rippon Tor, The Nutcracker was, until dislodged in the late 20th century, a logan or rocking stone. Five metres in length, over one metre square and weighing around

14 tonnes, the giant stone slab could be rocked with a single hand. *The Nutcracker* gained its name as – according to local folklore – people would use it to crack nuts. One suspects that the locals were more cracking a joke at the expense of outsiders.

Aside from exposed granite "tor" hilltops, around one-third of Dartmoor is covered with peat bogs, known as mires. *Fox Tor Mires* may have been the inspiration for Great Grimpen Mire in Sir Arthur Conan Doyle's detective novel, *The Hound of the Baskervilles*.

Dartmoor boasts the largest concentrations of stone rows of any area in Britain, with at least seventy. It also boasts the longest stone row in the world; but, as is often the case in life, there are problems worthy of bullet points:

- The stone row could be called either *Stalldown* or *Staldon*, although some websites refer to the stone row as *Upper Erme* or *Stall Moor*.

- It could be 2.12 miles in length, but then, as one website puts it, traced on Memory Map it comes to 2.75 miles.

- Spaced between 1.3 and 1.6 metres apart, there could be around 800 stones, although there may be as many as 917.

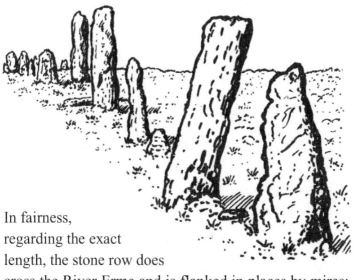

In fairness, regarding the exact length, the stone row does cross the River Erme and is flanked in places by mires; not the easiest place to visit with a trundle wheel. Orientated north to south, the northern terminal is marked by a cairn on Green Hill, the southern terminal by a stone circle known as *The Dancers*. The stone row may date to the Bronze Age, although it could be a lot older.

Close to Princetown, in the heart of the National Park, Dartmoor Prison opened in 1809 to house French prisoners captured during the Napoleonic Wars. Once regarded as high security and escape-proof, the prison today mainly houses non-violent white-collar criminals such as money launderers, forgers, cybercriminals and copyright infringers (note to self: before publication, check manuscript for copyright infringement!)

The prison is part of the estate of the Duchy of Cornwall.

Each summer *Dartmoor Prison Break* sees non-incarcerated participants "escape" and flee as far as possible in 24 hours. Movement of the "escapees" is monitored by GPS tracker and all funds raised from the event go to Dartmoor Search and Rescue Team Plymouth. Escapees have been tracked as far away as Somerset and the Lizard peninsular in Cornwall, a distance as the crow flies of over 60 miles. If you have ever felt the urge to escape from a prison, do not delay as Dartmoor Prison is scheduled for closure in 2023.

With no natural lakes on Dartmoor, Crazywell Pool, two miles south of Princetown and with a surface area the size of a football pitch, is thought to be either a shaft or reservoir related to a disused tin mine below Cramber Tor. Locals once believed that the pool was bottomless, recounting the tale of parishioners of either Walkhampton or Sheepstor using bell ropes from the local church to evaluate its depth. Knotted together and weighted at one end, they sank the ropes to over 80 fathoms, around 150 metres, without success. The legend met a watery end in 1844 when, during a dry summer, the Plymouth Dock Water Company drained the pool down to a few buckets of sludge to supplement the water supply of Devonport Leat. The "bottomless pool" was found to plunge to no more than 4.9 metres at its western end, its deepest point.

The locals, not to be put off by evidence, claim that the water rises and falls with the tides of the sea. Furthermore, at dusk a voice can be heard calling out across the water, announcing the name of the person who will be next to die in the parish, an image of their face reflected in the surface of the pool at midnight on

Midsummer's Eve. Others believe Crazywell Pool to be haunted by the Witch of Sheepstor, Oracle of the Pool, renowned for administering bad advice.

Dartmoor folklore also tells of a hunter named Bowerman. Chasing a hare, Bowerman and his pack of hounds stumbled upon a coven of witches, upending their cauldron and disrupting their sorcery. Taking umbrage, the next time Bowerman was hunting, one of the witches turned into a hare and lead the hunter and his hounds into a mire. Trapped and awaiting his fate, the witch conjured a spell and turned the hapless hunter to stone.

Taller than one might envisage, the stone – a granite stack the height of 1½ double decker buses on the northern slopes of Hayne Down, close to the village of Manaton – is known, due to its vaguely human-with-a-big-hooter profile, as *Bowerman's Nose*.

The hounds, suffering a similar stony fate, now form a cluster of rocks on the appropriately named *Hound Tor*. The legend of the canine origin of the granite outcrop is said to have inspired Sir Arthur Conan Doyle's *The Hound of the Baskervilles*, with Sherlock Holmes investigating reports of a demonic hound stalking the foggy moorland. The rocky tor features in the 2012 episode of *Sherlock*, starring Benedict Cumberbatch.

The *Beast of Dartmoor*, described as resembling a large black bear, is said to be seen walking close to Hound Tor.

Held annually on the second Saturday in September, Widecombe-in-the-Moor hosts a village fair, made popular by the rhyme...

Tom Pearce, Tom Pearce,
Lend me your grey mare,
All along, down along, out along, lee
For I want to go to Widecombe Fair
Wi' Bill Brewer, Jan Stewer, Peter Gurney,
Peter Davy, Dan'l Whiddon, Harry Hawke,
Old Uncle Tom Cobley and all,
Old Uncle Tom Cobley and all.

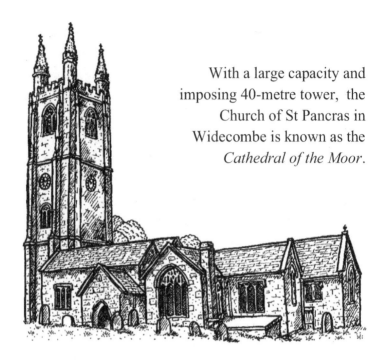

With a large capacity and imposing 40-metre tower, the Church of St Pancras in Widecombe is known as the *Cathedral of the Moor*.

In 1638, during what is remembered as the *Great Thunderstorm*, the 14th-century church was struck by ball lightening, the north-east pinnacle of the tower plunging into the nave and chancel. With afternoon service underway, four of the congregation were killed and a further sixty injured. According to folklore, during the service a gambler had fallen asleep; the Devil, wishing to claim his soul, tethered the gambler's horse to the pinnacle and hurled a fireball at the church, causing the frightened horse to bolt and the pinnacle to tumble.

The Devil features in many a Devonian tale, such as the tradition celebrated annually on 5 November of

Turning the Devil's Stone. At eight o'clock in the evening, a cacophony sounds throughout the village of Shebbear as bell-ringers sound a jarring peal from the tower of St Michael's Church. With the Devil hopefully kept at bay by the tuneless tune the discordant campanologists exit the church with crowbars in hand and make their way to the village green. Under an ancient oak tree on the green sits what is known locally as the *Devil's Stone*. As the vicar recites a prayer, the bell-ringers surround the stone and, shouting excitedly, turn it over.

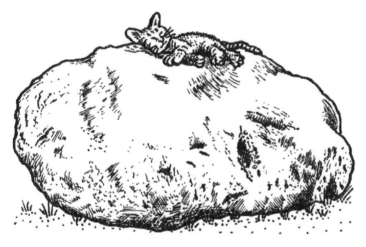

This turn of events began when the stone fell from the Devil's pocket as he fought with God, trapping him beneath it. Turning the stone annually ensures that his efforts to tunnel free remain fruitless, thereby saving the village from a potential disaster.

On more solid ground, geology suggests that the misplaced stone may have been deposited at the end of the last ice age; otherwise, it could be the remnant of either a standing stone, or an altar stone dating back to pagan times.

As the expression goes, never let the truth get in the way of a good story, and – returning to local legend – a further story tells that the boulder was quarried locally for use as the foundation stone for Henscott Church, to be built on the other side of the River Torridge at nearby Bradford, but the Devil kept bringing it back to Shebbear. Eventually, the builders gave up and left it there.

Either way, with the stone turned for another year, locals retire to the nearby Devil's Stone Inn for liquid refreshment.

Following a heavy snowstorm, over several nights in February 1855, a series of hoof-like footprints appeared in the snow around the estuary to the River Exe. Extending from Exmouth up to Topsham and across the estuary to Dawlish and Teignmouth, eyewitness accounts report that the prints continued unbroken over walls, houses, rivers and haystacks, leading up to and exiting narrow drainpipes en route. Estimates put the total distance covered at between 40 and 100 miles.

As hysteria grew with the belief that the tracks were left by the cloven hoof of the Devil, the local Reverend

G. M. Musgrave attempted to put people at ease with the suggestion that a couple of kangaroos had escaped from a private menagerie in Sidmouth. Given that kangaroos would struggle to crawl through drainpipes, other suggestions for the *Devil's Footprints* included hopping mice, badgers, and an experimental balloon with trailing ropes that had broken free from its mooring at the dockyard at Devonport.

Nestled on the River Otter east of Exeter is the town of Ottery St Mary. According to local legend, before the founding of the town, pixies occupied the hills, forests and meadows around the banks of the river. The pixies happily co-existed for thousands of years with prehistoric humans, who shared their pagan beliefs. That was until their peace was disturbed with the arrival of Celtic missionaries, vowing to spread Christianity. With civil unrest on the increase, things came to a head in 1454 when a set of bells were being raised into the tower of the newly built Christian Church of St Mary. The pixies did everything they could to interfere, all to no avail, as the bells were installed and rang out for the first time on Midsummer's Eve. The pixies fled to their Pixie's Parlour cave on the banks of the river, later creeping back into town to kidnap the bell-ringers. The bell-ringers escaped from imprisonment in the cave and returned to gain revenge by the ringing of the church bells.

And so, every year on the Saturday nearest to Midsummer's Day, the Cubs, Scouts and Guides of Ottery dress as pixies and re-enact the capture and later revenge of the bell-ringers. The day begins with the pixie hordes making an unholy racket in Broad Street before being addressed by the Chief Pixie, thereafter setting off to the church to capture the bell-ringers and parade them through the streets. The bell-ringers escape, the pixies flee the town and it all ends with a fireworks display.

If you doubt the truth of this story, Pixie's Parlour is a sandstone cave around one mile south of Ottery St Mary.

Wearing no more protection than oversized oven gloves, residents of Ottery St Mary also celebrate Guy Fawkes Night on 5 November by running a relay through the streets, each carrying aloft one of 17 flaming wooden barrels. The barrels are first lined with coal tar and stuffed with paper and straw, the highly inflammable contents then soaked in paraffin before the open end of the barrel set alight.

It sounds so inviting I would love to take part myself, were it not for my fear of oversized oven gloves.

Exeter, with a population of 130,000, is the county town of Devon.

Measuring 1.22 metres at its widest and 64 cm at its narrowest point, Parliament Street in Exeter claims to be the world's narrowest street. Built in the 14th century to connect the High Street to Waterbeer Street, Parliament Street was originally called Small Lane until renamed by Exeter Council as a way of mocking what they saw as the narrow-mindedness of Members of Parliament for passing the 1832 Reform Act. Under the act, Exeter would have lost its automatic entitlement to seats in parliament's House of Commons.

Five miles north-east of Exeter is the village of Broadclyst, and within the village is the neighbourhood of Dog Village; I don't imagine that Dog Village will thank me for mentioning that it has a street named *Slaparse Lane*. Other places in Devon with names worthy of a Christmas stocking filler book of humorous place names of Britain include *Inner Ting Tong* in the village of Knowle; *Knick Knack Lane* in Brixham (home to a Paddiwack Cottage); *Squeezebelly Lane* in Kingsbridge; Lickham Bottom, a valley south west of Hemyock; and *Bastard's Lane* in Great Torrington.

Moving swiftly on to sport, and *Devonian wraxling*, otherwise known as Devon wrestling, was once popular in the county. Comparable to how a conker becomes more lethal once baked, prior to fighting opponents would bake their boots, with the intention of later causing severe injury to their opponent. Wraxling died out in the 19th century as it was considered too deadly a sport.

Devon invented the cream tea; a statement guaranteed to provoke many a bunfight in the tearooms of neighbouring Cornwall. Written evidence suggests that, in the 11th century, monks in Tavistock's Benedictine Abbey fed workers undertaking restoration work, bread, clotted cream and strawberry jam. And, in answer to whether it is cream first, then the jam, or jam first... cream in Devon, jam in Cornwall.

Devon also invented the Cornish pasty! One might think the clue was in the name, excepting that more written evidence – this time a set of audited civic accounts for the Devon town of Plymouth dated 1509/10 – lists a pasty purchased for the princely sum of 10d – 4 pence in decimal currency. According to the Bank of England inflation calculator, which allows for a 1.4% consumer price increase per year, 10d in 1510 would be around £50 today, so I can only conclude that the pasty either contained Beluga caviar or the cost included delivery from some distance away; somewhere, perhaps, like Cornwall. I feel a Food Court would dismiss this "evidence" as vague and inconclusive. Furthermore, a quick flick through *The Official Encyclopaedia of the Cornish Pasty* tells of line drawings dated to 8,000 BC discovered in caves at the Lizard, the southern tip of Cornwall, depicting women eating pasties whilst their men are stag hunting. Then again, the evidence is inconclusive as the pasties have no pastry, the outer casing being leaves, albeit with crimped edges.

There are many more things about Devon that are worthy of a mention, and many notable people, including Sir Francis Drake, Sir Walter Rayleigh and

Agatha Christie; but, as said, Devon is the only county in England to have two separate coastlines. In tackling the South West Coast Path you will be walking the entirety of both of them, and I would not want this book to weigh down your rucksack, so I will save south Devon for when we get there.

Day 3
Lynmouth to Combe Martin

Distance: 13.7 miles
Ascent: 1,148 metres

Although the combined population of Lynton and Lynmouth is under 2,000, two-thirds live above the cliff, and Lynton, looking down upon its village neighbour, is officially a small town.

Should you set off before the Cliff Railway opens or hold the principle that riding a train for part of the route is cheating, you have a choice of three walking routes, all zigzagging up the cliff. The official route begins to the right of the National Park Centre on the Esplanade. Upon reaching the top, turn right and right again onto North Walk. The path takes you around Hollerday Hill, once the site of Hollerday House, the grand mansion home of Sir George Newnes, Lynton's major benefactor.

In 1881 Newnes founded the magazine *Tit-Bits from all the Interesting Books, Periodicals, and Newspapers of the World*, a mini-encyclopaedia more commonly known as *Tit-Bits*. Published weekly, the magazine provided snippets of information presented in an easy-to-read format – what could be described as the modern day *i* newspaper for pre-teenaged and working-class Victorians. The magazine paved the way for popular journalism, with Arthur Pearson, who won a job on the publication following a competition, launching the *Daily Express*, and Alfred Harmsworth, one of the magazine's contributors, founding the *Daily Mail*.

Tit-Bits was an enormous success, soon reaching a circulation of 700,000, and in 1891 Newnes began publication of *The Strand Magazine*, serializing his good friend Sir Arthur Conan Doyle's new mystery detective novels featured the exploits of Sherlock Holmes.

Having fallen in love with the Exmoor coastline and with his increasing fortune, Newnes set about building Hollerday House and spending his wealth on developing Lynton as a tourist destination. He was the driving force behind both the Funicular and the Lynton & Barnstaple Railway, along with funding the construction of many buildings, including the Congregational Church and the Town Hall.

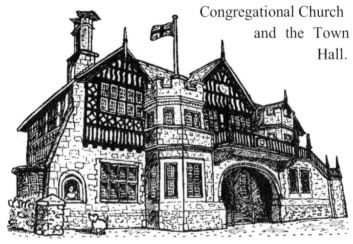

Establishing *Country Life* and several other publications, George Newnes is regarded as the founding father of popular journalism. He died in June 1910 aged 59, and is buried in Lynton Old Cemetery. A mysterious fire destroyed Hollerday House just three years later, and the army demolished the remains during the Second World War as part of a training exercise.

With trains travelling at 12 miles an hour, the narrow-gauge *Lynton & Barnstaple Railway* followed a 19-mile scenic route, crossing Chelfham Viaduct. At 121 metres in length and constructed using over 250,000 bricks, the viaduct is the largest structure built to serve narrow-gauge trains in Britain.

Although Chelfham Viaduct still stands today, the Lynton & Barnstaple Railway, struggling with falling passenger numbers due to improvement in road travel, eventually closed in 1935.

But the story does not quite reach the buffers; in 2004 a short section reopened as a heritage line, with

Victorian steam trains running between Woody Bay and Killington Lane, three miles west of Lynton, with long-term plans to reopen the entire route.

Photographs and models of the railway (along with plenty of local history) is on display at the *Lyn & Exmoor Museum*, housed in St Vincent's Cottage in Market Street. The cottage is Lynton's oldest surviving domestic dwelling.

Rounding Hollerday Hill, the coast path opens out to reveal views of Wringcliff Bay and the *Valley of Rocks*, described by Robert Southey as "the very bones and skeletons of the earth". A dry basin thought created by the River Lyn before changing course, the valley is edged with spectacular rock pinnacles, the most noticeable, to the right of the mini roundabout, being the towering mass of Castle Rock; the rock is named after the fortress-shaped formation crowning its 139-metre peak.

Across the valley from Castle Rock is the Devil's Cheesewring, a cheesewring being an old tool used to press cheese curd. They may well still stock them in Robert Dyas. Folklore tells that the Devil caught a group of unruly druids dancing in the valley on a Sunday, and a Sunday not being a day for merriment he turned them all to a stone, forming the shape of a cheesewring.

R. D. Blackmore in *Lorna Doone* recounted tales of Mother Meldrum's Kitchen, a witch's cave beneath the Cheesewring. Although a cave no longer exists, nearby in the valley is Mother Meldrum's Tea Room, should you be spitting feathers, AKA in need of refreshment.

To your left is Rugged Jack; as you pass, look back and you may spot the shapely image of the "White Lady" in Jack's cracks.

Below Rugged Jack is the *Lynton & Lynmouth Cricket Club*, more renowned (as it proudly announces on its website) for its picturesque playing venue than its cricketing achievement. Listen out for the joyful sound of a cricket ball hitting a willow bat.

Listen and look out also for the hardy herd of feral goats that cling to the rockfaces. Goats have lived in the Valley of Rocks on and off since prehistoric times, much photographed by visitors but often hated by locals as they've been known to headbutt sheep off the cliffs and escape over cattle grids, causing destruction to nearby land and property.

On the headland beyond Castle Rock is Duty Point Tower, a Victorian folly built on the estate of Lee Abbey. The folly, said to have been used by Customs & Excise patrols looking out for smuggling activity in the Bristol Channel, features in *Lonely Tower*, an 1879 etching by artist Samuel Palmer.

As you pass the arched gateway to Lee Abbey, Lee Bay comes into view, with Crock Point ahead and the headland of Wringapeak on the far side of Woody Bay. A little west of Wringapeak the path crosses Hollow Brook, a contender for both the highest coastal waterfall in the West Country and one of the highest waterfalls in Britain. From the hamlet of Martinhoe, Hollow Brook tumbles 210 metres down the hillside in a series of cascades, with two almost vertical 50-metre drops, before flowing into the sea.

At Highveer Point the path turns inland, dropping down to cross the River Heddon via a stone bridge. Toilets and refreshments are available at The Hunter's Inn, a short diversion south along the riverside path.

Crossing the bridge, the coast path zigzags up the hillside before following the contours seaward to Peter Rock, with steep views down to Heddon's Mouth. From Peter Rock the path heads westward, rising through the heather-covered slopes to the East Cleave headland, with views westward to Great Hangman and the distinctive pyramidal cone of Little Hangman.

You are now below the farmstead community of Trentishoe, notable for St Peter's Church. With a service held around four times a year for a congregation that struggles to reach double figures, the diminutive 15th-century parish church was no bigger than St Bueno's at Culbone until a chancel was added in 1861. Overlooking the pews at the rear of the church is a narrow musicians' gallery, so lacking in space that there is a hole cut in the wooden parapet to allow room for the bow of the double bass. The church's small organ in the gallery came from HMS Mauretania, once the world's fastest ocean liner, and hanging from the roof above the gallery is a colony of lesser horseshoe bats, a rare species that survive only in Wales and the West Country. The protected bats are not overly keen on the sound of a hoover and St Peter's struggles with the constant mess of bat droppings. It may be advisable to hold an open umbrella over your head when inside.

The coast path continues past the remains of Bronze Age hut circles below Trentishoe Down before following the contours seaward of Holdstone Down.

In 1958, Holdstone Down was visited by Dr George King, founder of the Aetherius Society, having received guidance from an undisclosed cosmic source advising him that he was to become the voice of Interplanetary Parliament. In the first "Great Mission of Operation Starlight" the former taxi driver was joined on the summit by the radiant form of the "Master Jesus", an extra-terrestrial being from the planet Venus. According to the society's website, the great Cosmic Avatar sent streams of spiritual power through Dr King, deep into the mountain itself, making Holdstone Down forever holy. A stone at the summit commemorates the event, with the date and Dr King's initials. If, looking up the hill, you see a gathering of people holding hands and uttering sacred verse, it may be members of the Aetherius Society, who hold regular pilgrimages to the sacred mountain to harvest cosmic energy and communicate with extra-terrestrial intelligence in the hope of resolving Earthly problems.

Continuing, Great Hangman comes into view across the valley. Peaking at 318 metres, the highest sea cliff in Devon is also the highest point on the South West Coast Path. Before you can reward your lofty achievement of scaling the path's highest point with a celebratory Devonshire pasty, the path first drops down to cross Sherrycombe.

According to a compelling story attributed to a German U-boat Commander by the name of Martens, during the Second World War German submarines operating in the Irish Sea and Bristol Channel would use the seclusion of Sherrycombe to land crew at night by dinghy to fill barrels with fresh water from the valley's waterfall.

Until 1875, Great Hangman's eastern and southern slopes were used for the opencast mining of manganese and iron ore. The remains of Girt Down Mine are still visible. Further inland, the underground shafts of Knap Down Mine extracted lead and silver, the silver used to fund the war expenses of King's Edward III and Henry V, with Combe Martin silver also used in the Royal collection of Crown Jewels.

From Great Hangman, the coast path gently slopes for one mile to Little Hangman, turning south before its distinctive peak to skirt between Lester Cliffs and the secluded Wild Pear nudist beach before dropping down into Combe Martin, the end of today's walk.

To misquote the Roman philosopher, Lucius Annaeus Seneca, it's not the length that matters... although in the case of Combe Martin, it has importance. Nestled in a narrow valley, the village spreads little further than one single long street, the street measuring two miles from the sheltered harbour to the village sign, and consequently is commonly referred to as the longest village street in England. Killjoys argue that the village sign is a long way up the valley from the start of the village, the longest village street claim being an embellishment of the fact that Combe Martin holds the Guinness World Record for the longest street party (that is, if you disallow the 37-mile-long party on the A40 motorway in Germany in 2010 on the grounds that a motorway is not a street.)

In 1690, after winning a considerable sum gambling at cards, George Ley, the local squire and owner of much of the land around Combe Martin, commissioned a house to be built that would forever remind him of his success. Mimicking the 4 suits, 13 cards in a suit and 52 cards in a pack of playing cards, Ley built his new house with 4 floors, 13 doors on each floor and with 52 steps and 52 windows.

Originally sitting on a 52-square-foot plot of land and with steep, angled roofs, the finished house resembled a giant house of cards.

Following George Ley's passing, the house later became the King's Arms Inn before changing its name in 1933 to the *Pack o'Cards*. Should you need refreshment following your descent from Great Hangman, the Pack o'Cards is half a mile from the beach, along Combe Martin's lengthy High Street. Plenty of other refreshment providers are available.

If you arrive in the village during the Spring Bank Holiday weekend you may see something odd going on. Do not be alarmed. Friday of the holiday weekend marks the start of the annual three-day celebration of *The Hunting of the Earl of Rone*.

Events begin with the "Earl", disguised in a suit of straw-stuffed sacking, with wooden "ship's biscuits" hung from his neck and face hidden behind a red, white and blue mask, attempting to evade capture from a band of fake Grenadier Guards.

Dressed in red tunics with black breeches, the Guards sport colourful pointy hats that resemble the remnants of children's Christmas paperchain decorations.

The fake Grenadiers are assisted in their search by local villagers, the women dressed in 19th-century "peasant" costume, the men dressed in breeches and smocks, with top hats, bowlers or flat caps. Bloodhounds they are not, as it is not until the Monday evening when two drummers lead the baying pack up to nearby Lady Wood, that the Earl, cornered hiding amongst the trees, is finally arrested. Dutifully seated backwards on a donkey, the captured prisoner is paraded along the High Street, pausing to be "shot" at intervals by his guards.

Falling dead to the floor and following revival by the "Fool", the Earl is helped back onto the donkey by a hobbyhorse, the horse inexplicably masquerading as a giant fairy cake. Upon reaching the beach he receives a final dummy bullet and falls to the sand, dead. The fake Grenadiers then wade into the water, tossing an effigy of the Earl out to sea.

The Hunting of the Earl of Rone is said to recount the fortunes of Sir Hugh O'Neill, the Earl of Tyrone, who opposed English rule in Ireland. Following defeat in the Nine Years' War, in 1607 the Earl fled his native Ireland, his journey ending shipwrecked on the north Devon coast in Rapparee Cove, west of Combe Martin. Surviving only on ship's biscuits, O'Neill hid from search parties in Lady Wood until captured by Grenadiers Guards.

Truth be known, fearing that their enemies were plotting their execution, O'Neill along with fellow Irish chieftains sailed to the safety of Spain. With the Earl of Tyrone failing to set foot on English soil, exactly why the villagers of Combe Martin celebrate the ancient tradition of The Hunting of the Earl of Rone has been lost to the misty seas of time.

Day 4
Combe Martin to Woolacombe

Distance: 13.9 miles
Ascent: 1,011 metres

As you leave Combe Martin, you also leave Exmoor, and the path, never straying too far from the old coast road, changes from woodland with rugged cliffs and buttress headlands to more open views and hidden coves. Close to Watermouth Valley Camping Park, the double-fronted cove of Broad Sands often tops the list of Devon's most beautiful hidden beaches. Accessed via 220 steep cliff steps, the secluded cove is neither broad nor overly sandy.

A little further on brings you to Watermouth Cove, a sheltered haven for small boats, shielded from the Atlantic waves by the headland of Sexton's Burrows. Halfway along the headland is a small round lookout tower, thought to be associated with Watermouth Castle. The mock-castle, ahead to your left, is a Gothic style country house commissioned in the 1820s by a Joseph Davie Bassett and wife Eleanora for the intended residence of their son Arthur and fiancée Harriet following their wedding. Although records are somewhat sketchy, according to the 1859 edition of *Murray's Handbook for Devon and Cornwall*, at the time of going to print the interior of the building was still not finished, by which time the not-so-newlyweds had been married for almost forty years and raised four children. Harriet died just four years later in 1863, Arthur surviving until the end of the decade before falling off his horse.

Used during the First World War as a convalescent home for wounded army officers, Watermouth Castle was again requisitioned in the Second World War as the headquarters for *Operation Pluto*, a double-acronym plan to lay **P**ipe-**L**ines **U**nder **T**he **O**cean to France for **P**ipe-**L**ine **U**nderwater **T**ransportation of **O**il in support of the Allied invasion of Normandy. In December 1942, in a full-scale rehearsal, a two-inch diameter pipe was laid 30 nautical miles under the choppy waters of the Bristol Channel from Watermouth to Swansea. Whilst plans for the invasion continued, the pipeline was used to pump oil from Wales to parts of Devon and Cornwall.

In August 1944, the first of 18 Pluto pipelines was laid from Shanklin Chine on the Isle of Wight, over 70 nautical miles along the bed of the English Channel to Cherbourg. Unfortunately, an escorting destroyer caught the line with its anchor and, following further teething problems, the pipeline was abandoned. A section of the pipe, three inches in diameter and clearly marked **P.L.U.T.O** in large letters, can still be seen at Shanklin Chine, while the oil pumping station, in the nearby resort of Sandown, was housed in a small building disguised as Brown's Ice Cream Parlour. The pumping equipment is still in place, the building now the Browns Family Golf clubhouse and cafe.

Watermouth Castle is now a theme park, with attractions including Gnome Land.

At most times, the coast path follows the southern edge of Water Mouth. At high tide, keep to the road until a stile on your right leads you through woodland and meadow to Widmouth Head. As you round the head, Lundy Island comes into view, 25 miles due west above Rillage Point.

The sea between here and Lundy is popular with basking sharks. Second only in size to whale sharks and bigger than the great white, adult basking sharks typically reach eight metres but can grow to over 10 metres. The longest recorded, having been trapped in a herring net off the coast of Canada in 1851, measured over 12 metres and weighed an estimated 16 metric tons, more than twice the weight of an African elephant.

Distinctive in appearance, with a gaping jaw lined with rows of teeth, they may look threatening but are harmless to humans, slow moving and appearing to bask on warmer surface water (hence their name) as they feed on zooplankton and small fish, filtered through their large gills.

Continue along the clifftop with views across Hele Bay to Ilfracombe, one mile ahead. Rounding Beacon Point, the path zigzags up Hillsborough, a local nature reserve topped by the ramparts of an Iron Age hill fort and the remains of a First World War gun battery. The name Hillsborough derives from Hele's Barrow, although the popular beauty spot is known locally as *The Sleeping Elephant*.

Looking down on Ilfracombe, on the quayside to the right of the small harbour, Damien Hirst's 20-metre-tall *Verity* sculpture is on loan to the town until 2032. Holding the traditional symbols of justice – a raised sword and a set of scales – the pregnant woman, devoid of flesh on one side and with her developing foetus exposed for all to see, is in the words of the artist, "a modern allegory of truth and justice". Others might call her an eyesore; I will let you be the judge.

From April until October, HMS Oldenburg sails to Lundy from Ilfracombe's quayside, departing at least three times a week; I would highly recommend a visit.

If you are walking in August, the quayside may well be packed with onlookers gathered to watch the annual

South West Birdman Competition, which sees competitors in fancy dress attempt to recreate the flight of a bird by launching themselves into the harbour.

Walkers in June may enjoy the *Ilfracombe Victorian & Steampunk Celebration*, with costumes, parades, tea parties, Bathing Belles, the Suffragettes March and much more.

Overlooking the harbour from the rocky mound of Lantern Hill, 14th-century St Nicholas' Chapel is Ilfracombe's oldest building. Built as a seamen's

chapel, a burning lantern in its window helped guide boats into the harbour. After losing its chapel status in 1540 when Henry VIII dissolved the monasteries, the building served as a laundrette before officially becoming a lighthouse in 1819. Still operational, St Nicholas' Chapel is said to be the UK's oldest working lighthouse. Atop the Grade I listed building is a charming copper fish weathervane.

In the distance behind St Nicholas' Chapel, the two white conical shapes that could from afar be mistaken for the chimneys of a coal-fired power station are the twin towers of the Landmark Theatre, constructed in 1997 and known locally as *Madonna's Bra*, a reference which may be lost on younger readers.

The big grass and rock headland to the right of Madonna's upper underwear is Capstone Hill. According to local legend, when the men of Ilfracombe were away fighting the French navy, their wives and girlfriends would climb to the top of the hill wearing red petticoats, so as to fool the French into thinking that there was a brigade of British Army "Redcoats" defending the town.

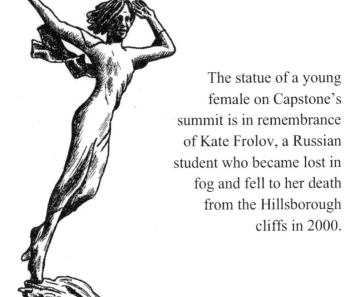

The statue of a young female on Capstone's summit is in remembrance of Kate Frolov, a Russian student who became lost in fog and fell to her death from the Hillsborough cliffs in 2000.

Descending towards the harbour, the coast path passes Rapparee Cove, a ladies' bathing beach in Victorian times. On a stormy night in October 1796 the transport ship *The London* was blown onto the cove's rocks and sank whilst trying to enter the harbour. According to the memorial stone, at least forty St Lucian prisoners of the Napoleon Wars were lost, along with local people who went to their aid.

To guide you through Ilfracombe, blue tile signs are set into the pavement. From the harbour, follow the signs along Capstone Road, leading to Capstone Parade and around the headland below Capstone Hill. Henry

Williamson, author of *Tarka the Otter*, lived below Capstone Hill in a small cottage in Capstone Road from the mid-1950s until 1976, a year before his death.

At Wildersmouth Beach, take the steps seaward of the Landmark Theatre to cross Jubilee Gardens into Granville Road. Seaward of Granville Road, secluded sandy coves were once only accessible by either climbing down the cliff face, swimming around the headland or clambering over rocks at low tide. In 1820, Welsh miners were engaged to dig four access tunnels to the coves, two of the tunnels leading to male and female segregated beaches, both with their own tidal pools. The Tunnels Beaches, as they became known, together with the arrival of the railway in 1874, led to a boom in tourism, Ilfracombe growing from a fishing village to a popular seaside resort. In accordance with Victorian morals, even though the beaches were segregated, women were still obliged to bathe in top-to-toe swimsuits, while the men would swim naked. The entrance to the tunnels, which run below Granville Road, is opposite Bath Place.

Veer right onto Torrs Walk Avenue and before long the path zigzags up The Torrs, known locally as the Seven Hills, with its spectacular clifftop views. At Torrs Point a toposcope designed by students from Ilfracombe Arts College points directions to local landmarks. Inland of

The Torrs is the distinctive spire of Holy Trinity Church. In the churchyard is the family grave of Hannibal Richards, a notorious smuggler from the village of Lee, ahead of you on the walk.

Guidebooks describe the stretch of coast between Ilfracombe and Woolacombe as rugged and inhospitable, with telling names such as Breakneck Point, an outcrop of jagged rocks below The Torrs. What does invite hospitality, nestled in a sheltered wooded valley a little further along the coast, is the village of Lee, where you will find welcome refreshments at the Grampus Inn; a grampus, as you may determine by the pub sign, being a species of dolphin.

In the 19th century, gardeners planted the walls of The Grange, a former manor house in Lee, with fuchsias; with the valley's sheltered temperate climate, the fuchsias spread throughout the village, and today it is known as Fuchsia Valley. Landscape artist Samuel Palmer painted the extraordinarily atmospheric *View of Lee* in 1835, which hangs in the Fitzwilliam Museum in Cambridge; prints are available to buy online, should you eventually find an internet signal.

In the 18th and early 19th centuries, the remoteness of this stretch of coast made Lee Bay ideal for smuggling activity. According to one report held at the National Maritime Museum in Greenwich, in June 1786 a Customs officer by the name of Edmund Fishley discovered a prize haul of contraband in John Beer's outhouse. The haul included 13 gallons of Portuguese red wine, 66 bottles of gin and a box containing 73 packs of playing cards, all missing the Ace of Spades.

Lee's most famous resident was Hannibal Richards, a member of the notorious Cruel Coppinger's smuggling gang in Morwenstow, north Cornwall. With authorities closing in on the gang, in 1789 Richards fled to Lee, where he lived at The Gwythers, at the time a farmhouse. He soon returned to his smuggling activities, evading capture until eventually retiring following the arrest of his fellow gang members.

The outdoor life and temperate climate served his family well, as Richards lived to the age of 85, his wife Jane lived to 101 and daughter, also named Jane, to 100 years and 6 months.

From Lee Bay the coast path rises above Damage Cliff (another name not inspiring confidence) before continuing to Bull Point and from there, Morte Point. The silvery-grey rocks below are Morte Slate, part of a narrow formation that runs east across north Devon and forms the Brendon Hills in Somerset. The jagged rocks create deadly reefs and this stretch of coast has seen countless shipwrecks, with five ships lost in the winter of 1852 alone; the word morte is French for dead, and Morte Point's literal translation is *Point of Death*.

According to folklore, this stretch of coast was also popular with wreckers, who would shine lanterns to lure ships onto the rocks and then plunder the cargo from the wreckage. As it was illegal to plunder from a wreck if its crew were still alive, the wreckers would first do away with any survivors. Eventually, in 1879 a lighthouse was built at Bull Point. The lighthouse survived until September 1972, when 30 metres of the cliff face subsided, leading to the fog signal station partly collapsing and cracks appearing in the building's walls.

The current
lighthouse
dates to 1974.

Legend tells that Grunta Beach, to the south of Morte Point, gained its name as a ship carrying a cargo of live pigs ran aground on the rocks of the small cove. Most of the pigs survived, one living on seaweed for a year.

As you round Morte Point, the north Devon coast comes into view, stretching 17 miles as the gull flies to the distant headland of Hartland Point. Continuing seaward of the village of Mortehoe leads you into Woolacombe, the end of today's walk.

Woolacombe derives from *Wolnecoma*, or *Wolves Valley*, a reference to what was once a valley dense with trees and a pack of large furry quadrupeds. The popular seaside resort's non-wolf population, when the tourists have left, is only one thousand.

Woolacombe today is known for its three-mile-long sandy beach. With its resemblance to Omaha Beach in Normandy, during the Second World War the US Army used the sand dune backed beach to practise amphibious landing assaults in preparation for the D-Day invasion. On the grass above the northern end of the beach, what appears to be two granite standing stones is a tasteful memorial dedicated to the US soldiers based in the area.

Lundy Island

Picture a map of the British Isles, remove Wales and flip it so that the West Country is in the east, and there you have Lundy, an island that loosely resembles a flipped map of England and Scotland in miniature. Three miles top-to-toe and 0.6 miles wide, rising to 143 metres at Beacon Hill; 1,100 acres of granite and slate, around 850 football pitches. A designated Site of Special Scientific Interest; one of only three Marine Nature Reserves in the UK; one of only three Marine Conservation Zones in the UK that have "no-take" protection banning fishing; and one of the largest seabird breeding colonies in the UK. Locations relating to Lundy's rich marine and bird life include Seals' Rock, Gannets' Rock and Puffin Slope.

As a popular migration route stop-off, Lundy is most famous for the puffin, the island's name derived from *Lundi* and *ey*, Old Norse words for puffin and island. In recognition of its name, post from the island carries special puffin postage stamps. The stamp charge, known as puffinage, was originally a local carriage label to cover costs incurred in transporting mail to the mainland. Stamps were placed top left, with a further stamp with the head of the monarch top right. Since 1974, puffinage covers costs to the mail's end destination, with no second stamp required.

Puffins have thrived on Lundy since the eradication in 2006 of black rats, which had preyed on the birds' eggs since arriving as stowaways on ships. A testament to Lundy's former rodent population is Rat Island, accessible at low tide by crossing the invitingly named Hell's Gate. Other inviting and curious names on the island include the Devil's Limekiln, Mermaid's Hole, Dead Cow Point and The Cheeses.

There are three walls that cross Lundy: the Quarter Wall, the Halfway Wall and the Threequarter Wall. Between the Quarter Wall and Halfway Wall runs a rock fracture called *The Earthquake*; geologists suggest the crack may be related to either mining activity or, more dramatically, the Great Lisbon Earthquake of 1755.

During the Second World War, two German Heinkel bombers crashed on the island. Parts of one remain just south of Halfway Wall.

Lundy is also a top diving destination, with more than 100 shipwrecks submerged close to its shores. One of the most popular is HMS Montague, which ran aground in May 1906 near Shutter Rock. Much of the Royal Navy battleship was salvaged but armour plate and 12-inch shells are still on the seabed.

The Lundy pony is a tough and hardy breed that has lived on the island since 1928, when mares and foals were introduced from the New Forest to mate with a stallion from the Welsh mountains.

Lundy cabbage is native to the island, a protected species that grows only on the more sheltered eastern cliffs and slopes. From May to August, the cabbage blossoms with yellow flowers that resemble oilseed rape. Despite an unwelcome taste described as "triple-distilled essence of Brussels sprout", two species of beetles feed on the cabbage – the Lundy cabbage flea beetle and the Lundy cabbage weevil.

Lundy's permanent population is 28, including the island's manager, a ranger and a warden, a farmer and the staff of the Marisco Inn, the island's only pub. The pub's name relates to the Marisco family, owners, or at least occupiers of Lundy until Henry II granted the island to the Knights Templar in 1160. The Mariscos returned following King John's accession to the throne in 1199. In 1235, William de Marisco was implicated in the murder of Henry Clement, a messenger of Henry III. The king sent troops to arrest him along with 16 of his followers, and in 1242 he was hung, drawn and quartered for treason.

With a tidal range of 8.2 metres and a fast-flowing current, ships are forced to navigate close to Lundy, and given its prominent location in the Bristol Channel, Henry III built a castle, now known as Marisco's Castle.

For many centuries, the commanding position made Lundy popular with pirates, who preyed on passing merchant ships, plundering their valuable cargos. From 1627 to 1632, Lundy was occupied by the *Sale Rovers*, a notorious band of Barbary Pirates from the Republic of Sale, a city state that is now part of Morocco. Lead by renowned Dutch renegade, Jan Janszoon, the pirates seized Europeans and transported them to Algiers to be sold as slaves.

In 1743, at the age of 37, Thomas Benson inherited the family fortune, along with a small fleet of ships. At the time it was government policy to deport convicted criminals to the American colonies, and Benson continued with the family's deportation business, using the ships to transport convicts, along with Irish linen, pewter and other valuable goods, across the Atlantic to Maryland and Virginia, returning with tobacco. Awarded the position of High Sheriff of Devon, Benson used his influence to enter politics and was dutifully elected MP for Barnstaple. In debt to Customs & Excise over unpaid import duties, Benson took to offloading tobacco on Lundy to avoid paying further tax. He also took to offloading convicted criminals, pocketing the fees for their deportation and using the unpaid labourers to work for him on the island. Aside from building the Quarter Wall, the non-deported criminals are credited with digging out what is now known as Benson's Cave.

And there began Benson's greatest fraud: in 1752, his barely seaworthy Brigantine ship *Nightingale* set sail from Barnstaple loaded with its usual cargo of linen, pewter and convicted criminals, en route to Maryland. The ship, under the command of Captain Lancey, docked at Lundy and, under cover of darkness, the crew offloaded the cargo, hiding it in the cave. The ship continued its journey, sailing west for 50 miles until Lancey sighted another ship, the *Charming Nancy*, whereupon the Nightingale was set alight and scuttled. As the ship sank, the crew were transferred to the Charming Nancy and transported to the safety of Clovelly Harbour. Benson's intention had been to claim on insurance for the loss of the Nightingale and its cargo, but the deception unravelled when one of the crew confessed. Captain Lancey was tried and executed for his part and Benson fled to Portugal, where he lived in exile.

In 1775, Lundy was sold to Sir John Borlase Warren for the sum of £10. When Warren left to fight in the War of American Independence the island was bought at auction by Sir Bart Vere Hunt, persuaded by the auctioneer's proclamation that Lundy was free from payment of tithe or tax, nor was accountable to King or Church. With the misguided belief that he was now owner of an Independent State, Hunt established a small Irish colony, declaring (although I can find no paper evidence to back this up) its own Constitution and issuing coinage and stamps.

Hen and Chickens
Seals' Rock
Puffin Slope
Old Copper Mine
Gannets' Rock
Devil's Slide
Frenchman's Landing
Threequarter Wall
Tibbetts
Gull Rock
Half Wall
Jenny's Cove
The Cheeses
Pondsbury
Dead Cow Point
Earthquake
Old Hospital
The Battery
Quarter Wall
Old Lighthouse
Ladies Beach
Mouse Island
Marisco Tavern
St Helena's
Rat Island
Shutter Point
Mermaid's Hole

A tale less believable than undertaking a 60-mile drive to test your eyesight is the story that, in 1830, two gentlemen by the names of John Matravers and William Striffe won Lundy from the Vere Hunt family in a game of cards; they actually bought it for £4,500.

In 1834, the "Independent State" of Lundy passed into the ownership of William Hudson Heaven, who dubbed his summer retreat *The Kingdom of Heaven*. In 1924, the island was sold to Martin Coles Harman, who promptly proclaimed himself *King of Lundy*, issuing Half Puffin and One Puffin coins, an action that lead to his prosecution under the 1870 Coinage Act. The coins are now valuable collectors' items.

Eventually, in 1969, philanthropist businessman Jack Hayward, concerned for the future preservation of the island, bought Lundy and donated it to the National Trust; the National Trust in turn leased it to The Landmark Trust. The Landmark Trust continue to manage and maintain the island, financed by visitors. On that note, although not part of the South West Coast Path, I would highly recommend a day's detour. During the holiday season, HMS Oldenburg makes the crossing from both Ilfracombe and Bideford, whilst out of season a helicopter service departs from Hartland Point.

Day 5
Woolacombe to Braunton

Distance: 14.9 miles
Ascent: 375 metres

Woolacombe Beach was gifted to the National Trust in 1909 by Rosalie Chichester, who lived at Arlington Court, a grand Neoclassical Regency country house ten miles inland on the edge of Exmoor. If you enjoy the sounds of the surf and sand under your feet, you may wish to walk along the length of Woolacombe and Putsborough Beaches to the Baggy Point headland. Officially, the coast path passes through the dunes to join Marine Drive, following the gorse-covered clifftop slopes below Woolacombe Down.

A little over a mile inland from Putsborough Beach is the village of Georgeham, mentioned in the Domesday Book as *Hama*, the *George* added following the building of St George's Church. Acclaimed author Henry Williamson is buried near the church's tower. From 1921, Williamson lived next to the church in Skirr Cottage, marrying his wife Ida in 1925. It was in Skirr Cottage that he wrote *Tarka the Otter*. Published in 1927, Tarka won the *Hawthornden Prize for Literature* the following year, the £100 prize together with £25 of savings allowing the couple to buy a plot of land overlooking Georgeham at Ox's Cross. Together with building a house on the plot, Williamson built a wooden hut nearby, where he spent up to 15 hours a day writing. Because of its historical interest, English Heritage has since awarded the hut Grade II listing.

Passing Putsborough Beach, the path turns west to round Baggy Point. The Upper Devonian Sandstone cliffs around the headland are a designated Site of Special Scientific Interest. In summer, brilliant yellow Hottentot figs carpet much of the headland; later in the season the leaves fade to pink.

Hottentot figs are an invasive species, introduced from South Africa by Victorian gardeners who were unaware that they spread like wildfire. The figs are currently listed under Schedule 9 of the *Wildlife and Countryside Act 1981*, awaiting eradication.

On the plus side, the leaves are edible, although you may prefer to wait until reaching one of the many eateries around the headland in Croyde for some non-invasive local food.

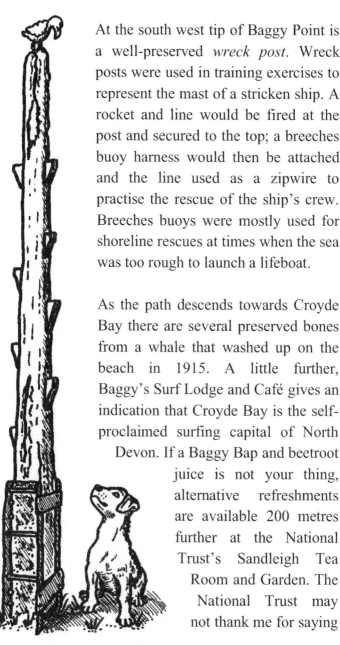

At the south west tip of Baggy Point is a well-preserved *wreck post*. Wreck posts were used in training exercises to represent the mast of a stricken ship. A rocket and line would be fired at the post and secured to the top; a breeches buoy harness would then be attached and the line used as a zipwire to practise the rescue of the ship's crew. Breeches buoys were mostly used for shoreline rescues at times when the sea was too rough to launch a lifeboat.

As the path descends towards Croyde Bay there are several preserved bones from a whale that washed up on the beach in 1915. A little further, Baggy's Surf Lodge and Café gives an indication that Croyde Bay is the self-proclaimed surfing capital of North Devon. If a Baggy Bap and beetroot juice is not your thing, alternative refreshments are available 200 metres further at the National Trust's Sandleigh Tea Room and Garden. The National Trust may not thank me for saying so, but if you sit in the walled garden and there is a whiff in the air, it may be coming from the sewage treatment works on the other side of the wall. If you happen to have a stepladder or periscope you will see that the treatment works is cleverly disguised to look like farm outbuildings. Edging National Trust land and serving a population that expands from a little over 1,000 to around 5,500 in the summer months, when built in 1994 the sewage works won an architectural award for its design. Once fully biologically treated, wastewater is released one mile out to sea via the Baggy Point outfall pipe. The bubbles offshore may not be coming from marine life after all.

Alongside Croyde Sewage Treatment Works is a small nature area for common toads to rest and relax en route to the artificial lake inland of the sand dunes at Croyde Beach; the lake is a nationally important breeding ground for the common toad.

An engaging story tells that Croyde takes its name from Crydda, a Viking raider who ruled the bay and surrounding area from around 794 AD. To repeat a quote often misattributed to Mark Twain, *never let the*

truth get in the way of a good story, and the story goes that, when the King of England declared that he owned all land above the low tide mark, Crydda was not best pleased as he could not legally moor and unload his Viking long ships. After seeking Royal council, the king agreed that as a privilege Crydda could own the beach between the low and high tide marks. With no documentary evidence to suggest that this has since been revoked, it appears that although much of the surrounding land above the high tide mark is owned by the National Trust, the sand between high and low tide on Croyde Bay Beach may still be owned by Crydda, ruler of the Vikings.

For those who enjoy phallic related humour, the upstanding boulder on Croyde Beach is Cock Rock. At low tide it may be easier to take the "Viking route" to cross the beach, although officially the path passes along the base of Croyde Burrows, an area of sand dunes stabilised with marram grass. If taking the dune route, stick to the paths as the area is a protected adder breeding ground.

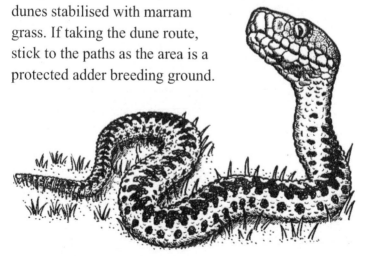

At the southern end of the beach the path turns seaward, continuing over rocks, across a small beach and up a flight of steps. As the expanse of Saunton Sands comes into view, the path leads up further steps to join the coast road by the old coastguard lookout station.

To the right of the lookout station, unfinished at the time of writing, is Chesil Cliff House, a new build designed to resemble a lighthouse. Construction of the house, which featured on TV in an episode of Grand Designs, ground to a halt in 2018 when the money ran out.

After first turning left, cross over and then follow the contours above the road to round the headland. At the Saunton Sands Hotel, the official route once again crosses the road to reach the beach. For those interested in rock formations, wedged below the cliffs to the north of the beach is the famous *Saunton Pink Erratic*, a 12-tonne pink boulder, thought to have been carried down from the highlands of Scotland in the last Ice Age.

The path immediately leaves the beach, passing behind houses and re-joining the road for 300 metres before turning right after the golf course entrance. The alternative route-with-a-view zigzags uphill and bypasses the road.

Along with Woolacombe, Putsborough and Croyde beaches, during the Second World War the US Army used Saunton Sands to practise amphibious landing assaults in preparation for the D-Day invasion. The Allied invasion is marked each June with a display of military vehicles, battle re-enactment and planes landing on the beach.

Stretching for over three miles, Saunton Sands has proved a popular cinematic backdrop; its film credits include *A Matter of Life and Death*, *Edge of Tomorrow*, and *Pink Floyd – The Wall*. It also appears, covered with over 700 wrought iron hospital beds, on the cover of Pink Floyd's 1987 album *A Momentary Lapse of Reason*.

Behind Saunton Sands is Braunton Burrows, three square miles of sand with dunes over 30 metres high, England's largest dune system. Aerial views showing the sheer scale of the Burrows can be seen in the music videos for both Robbie Williams' *Angels* and Olly Murs' *Hand on Heart*. Aside from being a Designated Area of Outstanding Natural Beauty, Braunton Burrows is the centre of the North Devon UNESCO Biosphere Reserve. The Reserve, covering 55 square miles from the catchment basins of the River Taw and River Torridge and out to sea to include Lundy Island, was established in 1976 to create a balance between conservation, learning and research, and sustainable development. It includes 671 Country Wildlife Sites, 63 Sites of Special Scientific Interest, four Local Nature

Reserves and at least one cleverly-disguised-as-a-barn-conversion sewage works.

The Burrows supports a diversity of plants, including sea holly, sea cabbage, sea rocket and sea spurge.

Crossing the golf course, the coast path joins the American Road, an old jeep track used by US troops during D-Day training exercises. The track marks the edge of the southern area of Braunton Burrows, still used by the Ministry of Defence for live ammunition training. At Crow Point, a detour west along a board walk crosses the sand dunes to The Neck, the southern tip of Saunton Sands and the start of the River Taw estuary. Across the estuary is Northam Burrows Country Park and the picturesque fishing village of Appledore, both part of tomorrow's walk. Retrace your steps and continue through the car park to Crow Beach House.

The path continues seaward of the house, following the estuary along the Great Sea Bank to round Horsey Island. The bank was built in 1811, along with a series of drainage channels and sluice gates, enclosing and draining the marshland. Horsey is an important winter stop-off for migrating birds.

At Pill's Mouth (*Pill* is a local name for a waterway or creek), the coast path turns north to follow the western bank of the River Caen. In 1854, the upper part of the Caen was straightened and banks added to create the Braunton Canal. Continue north along the canal bank, passing Velator Quay, once a thriving port, to the oversized village of Braunton, the end of today's walk.

Once refreshed, should you wish to learn some local agricultural history the Braunton Countryside Centre has an exhibition on Braunton Great Field, an exceptionally rare 350-acre medieval open-field farming system still being traditionally cultivated. Enclosed by the Great Hedge, the Great Field is divided into hundreds of unenclosed strips, known as *furlongs*; the strips are separated by unploughed turf balks, or *landshares*, with large pebble *bondstones* marking the end of each strip. The best view of the Great Field and Great Hedge is from the great mound of nearby rock known as West Hill.

For those on a different wavelength, Braunton is also home to the award-winning Museum of British Surfing.

Day 6
Braunton to Instow

Distance: 12.8 miles
Ascent: 13 metres

Today's walk is as flat as a pancake in a trouser press. From Braunton, return to the coast path and follow the disused railway line east along the north bank of the River Taw estuary. Running between Barnstaple and Ilfracombe, what was originally the *London & South Western Railway* branch line once carried glamorous sounding trains such as the Devon Belle and Atlantic Coast Express. With passenger numbers declining, the line closed in 1970.

On your right is HMB Chivenor, since 1995 a Royal Marine Base. Originally a civil airfield, from 1940 Chivenor served as an RAF Central Command Station and is now home to several serving units, including the No. 624 Volunteer Gliding Squadron RAF.

In 2011, Chivenor featured in the BBC TV series *The Choir: Military Wives*, with Gareth Malone forming a choir of wives and partners of personnel on active service in Afghanistan. The choir's song, *Wherever You Are*, topped the UK Christmas Singles Chart, holding off a strong challenge from Lou Monte's 1960 recording of *Dominick the Donkey*.

Follow the former railway line for five miles, passing under the bypass bridge before the tarmac path terminates at Barnstaple. The earliest recorded name for Barnstaple was *Beardstapolitum*, the *Beard* referring to the Viking bearded axe, with *stapol* meaning market. The market in question is Pannier Market, open every day except Mondays in a grand high-glass and timber-roofed Victorian building 98 metres long, running the length of Butchers Row. The ten shops of Butchers Row were originally all butchers; now just one butcher remains, along with a baker; sadly, no candlestick maker; nor a shop selling Viking bearded axes.

To combat Viking raids in the 9th century, Alfred the Great developed a network of roads and fortified settlements, known as *burhs*. As a burh, Barnstaple was allowed its own mint, and coins have been uncovered dating to the reign of Eadwig, England's king from 955 to 959. The *Museum of Barnstaple & North Devon* has on display an 11th-century silver penny, minted in Barnstaple during the reign of Cnut the Great, Danish King of England from 1016 until his death in 1035.

Cnut the Great was otherwise known as King Canute, derided for his failed attempt to demonstrate that he had the power to hold back the tide; rather apt as the tide in Barnstaple and north Devon rises and falls by up to eight metres. Of course, Canute was really attempting to demonstrate that his power was nothing compared to the supreme power God held over nature and the elements.

In 1844, fossils from a rare straight-tusked elephant were unearthed in Summerland Street in Barnstaple; the elephants roamed Europe and the UK until their extinction around 115,000 years ago. Tusk and bone fragments are displayed at the museum, alongside a full-size recreation of the front half of the Barnstaple Elephant.

Barnstaple Museum borders a triangular-shaped area known as The Square. In the middle of The Square, the Grade II-listed Albert Clock is a memorial to Prince Albert, the late husband of Queen Victoria. Built in 1862, from the time of its first unveiling the clock was known as the "four-faced liar", as each of its four successive faces was one minute behind the last. When the clock was overhauled in 2010, in keeping with time-honoured tradition, the four faces were once again set to varying times. When the clock stopped in 2017, the town clerk commented that, until repaired, at least Albert was "still right eight times a day".

To the east of The Square, Litchden Street is one of the oldest streets in Barnstaple. The Penrose Almshouses in Litchden Street were built in 1627 from a legacy left by John Penrose, a local cloth merchant. In his will, Penrose stipulated that each of the 20 houses must only be occupied by two people of the same sex, and that inhabitants should be local, God fearing and teetotal. At one end of the almshouses is a chapel and at the other a meeting room. The door of the meeting room still has musket holes dating back to the start of the English Civil War in 1642.

With a population of 24,000, Barnstaple is north Devon's largest town. Before the River Taw silted up, the town was a thriving river port known for manufacturing and exporting wool, and later importing tobacco from the North American colonies.

Following alongside the river, the coast path passes Queen Anne's Walk, confusingly not a walk but a fancy colonnaded building that was formerly The Mercantile Exchange, now a café. Before being filled in, the grass and paved area in front of the café was once the Quay, where ships docked to load and unload their merchandise.

Between the central colonnades of Queen Anne's Walk is a *Tome Stone*. Merchants would trade by placing their money on the stone, agreeing a price and then shaking hands before a witness. The flat-topped stone is called a *nail*, and said to be the origin of the expression *pay on the nail* or *cash on the nail*, meaning immediate payment without delay. As plausible as it sounds, especially given that the Tome Stone does vaguely resemble a giant nail, the expression originated from the Anglo-Norman *payer sur le ungle*, *ungle* deriving from the Latin *ungula*, meaning claw or nail; the expression meaning to pay by hand.

Next to Queen Anne's Walk is the Old West Gate. If you happen to arrive in Barnstaple on the Wednesday before 20th September you may spot a procession led by several Exmoor Horn sheep stopping at the Old West Gate, where the Town Clerk will read out an ancient proclamation. The procession is part of the *Proclamation of the Ancient Fair* ceremony conducted at the Guildhall to mark the start of Barnstaple Fair, a four-day event held on Seven Brethren Bank, south of the bridge. During the ceremony, a large white glove decorated with flowers and ribbons is suspended over the street from the Guildhall. The glove symbolises the open hand of friendship to those attending the fair. The ceremony dates to around AD 930, when Barnstaple received its Charter of Rights.

To the north of the town centre, Pilton was once an ancient and historic village, separated from Barnstaple by the marshy meanderings of the River Yeo. Now a suburb, each July Pilton hosts the *Green Man Festival*, starting with a parade that heads north across Long Bridge. Leading the parade is the Green Man (or woman, it is hard to tell), an ancient symbol of nature and fertility, walking on stilts with large elf shoes, floral trousers and their upper body shrouded in an unruly privet hedge adorned with flowers.

Accompanying the Green Man are two people, both in robes that appear to be made of tissue paper, one in red carrying a pole topped with a large red papier-mâché mask, and one in green carrying a pole with a large green mask topped with a wig made from a giant floor mop.

Following the mask-carriers are musicians, drummers, the Grim Reaper, the Town Crier and various others in fancy dress.

Outside the Parish Church of St Mary in Pilton, the characters perform a play, with the Green Man meeting the "Prior of the Benedictine Priory of Pilton" before being accepted into the Christian church.

At 159 metres, the Long Bridge is one of the longest medieval bridges in Britain. Information on the date of its construction is a bit woolly, although it is said that work began when two spinster sisters aided by local children spun the first two piers from cotton. A Will dated 1274 left a legacy for its upkeep. The bridge was severely damaged during the Civil War, repaired and widened in 1796 and widened again in 1963 to add footpaths on either side.

Speaking of footpaths, to resume today's walk, cross the Long Bridge, turn right and keep your eyes peeled for signposts leading you under the bypass bridge onto the disused *North Devon Railway Line*, now a tarmac cycle track and part of the Tarka Trail. The path continues along the southern edge of the Taw estuary to Fremington Quay.

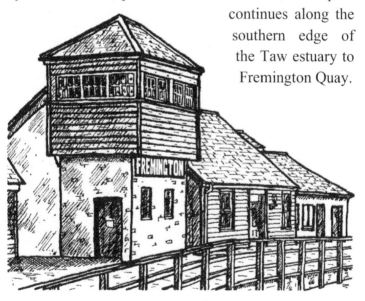

From early in the 19th century, silting in the River Taw, along with the building of bigger ships, increasingly rendered Barnstable's quay unusable. The solution was to construct a new, deep-water quay at Fremington, with a horse-drawn rail link to transport the cargo to and from Barnstaple. With the railway line opening in 1848, Fremington Quay was an immediate success, importing, amongst many things, coal, limestone and gravel, and exporting Devon ball clay to Europe for the manufacture of toilets. Much of the Quay and railway sidings has been restored, including the stationmaster's house, signal box, water tower and old lime kilns. The old station building is now a café (which I much appreciated the day I walked this stretch as it was hammering down with rain). The building also houses a Heritage Centre, with photos and exhibits portraying the Quay's industrial history, whilst a set of stairs leads to the signal box, with excellent views across the river.

Following Fremington's success, in 1855 the rail line was extended to run a passenger service to Bideford.

Once refreshed, continue along what was the *Bideford Extension Railway* to East Yelland Marsh, where the coast path turns right to follow a dyke past Isley Marsh Nature Reserve and Yelland Quay, site of a former power station. Across the river is Great Sea Bank and Horsey Island, part of yesterday's walk. When the tide is out the mudflats are popular with feeding birds. The path ahead is dependent on the tide, the low-tide route taking you down a set of steps and around the headland foreshore, at high tide passing behind the cricket ground. The headland marks the meeting point of the River Taw and the River Torridge, with views across the Taw to Braunton Burrows and the Torridge to Northam Burrows Country Park and Appledore. Both routes lead into Instow, the end of today's walk.

Aside from a decent beach and plenty of opportunities for refreshment, for me the highlight of Instow is the Grade II-listed signal box, which is open to the public on occasional Sundays and Bank Holidays during the summer.

Day 7
Instow to Westward Ho!

Distance: 11 miles
Ascent: 163 metres

In a 2009 episode of the TV series *James May's Toy Stories*, the ex-Top Gear presenter and his team attempted to create the world's longest model train set by laying 45,000 sections of miniature track along the 9.89 miles of disused railway line from Barnstaple to Bideford. With the track electrified using 160 car batteries, all was going well until the OO-scale Hornby Class 395 Javelin train proved to be less of a javelin and more of a shot put, its engine burning out at Instow.

Unlike the North Devon Railway Line, which was axed under the notorious Beeching cuts in the 1960s, *James May's Toy Stories* returned for a special episode in 2011, with May making a second attempt, this time in competition with the German engineers behind Miniature Wonderland model railway in Hamburg. According to 2016 figures, Miniature Wonderland has 1,300 trains, 10,000 carriages, 100,000 moving vehicles and 9.5 miles of track, so the engineers knew their stuff. All very well, but in the UK take pride in measuring systems that confound the rest of the world – yards, feet and inches; stones, pounds and ounces; gallons, quarts and pints – to name but a few. Drams, pecks, demijohns, bushels, firkins, kilderkins, yards-of-ale and a baker's dozen, to name but a few more. And when it comes to model railways, the UK is the only country to use OO scale; the rest of the world, Germany included, use the smaller HO scale. In model railway engineering, it appears that size matters, James May and his team's Hornby Inter-City 125 steamed through Instow and was the first to arrive in Bideford.

The coast path continues along the disused railway line, in two miles passing under the Torridge Bridge, carrying traffic on the A39 Atlantic Highway. The bridge opened in May 1987 and the following year cemented its place in history by winning the coveted *Concrete Society Award*.

Ahead, not unlike buses, just when you have walked for five days to find a medieval bridge, a second one comes into view; and they are both called *Long Bridge*, excepting that Bideford's is even longer than Barnstaple's, by all of 47 metres. At 206 metres, Bideford's Long Bridge is heralded as the second longest medieval bridge in England, the longest being Swarkestone Bridge in Derbyshire, This Derbyshire claim is at best dubious as most of Swarkestone Bridge's almost one-mile length is a causeway, plus the actual bridge section across the river was rebuilt after being destroyed by floods in 1795, making it a Georgian replica. To counter the argument, the first Long Bridge at Bideford was built of wood in 1286, with a stone replacement built around the timber in 1474 and a second stone bridge built on top of the first one in 1535. The medieval period ended in the 15th century, so is Bideford's Long Bridge also a replica?

Aside from having a medieval Long Bridge in common with Barnstaple, Bideford also has a Pannier Market with a glass and timber roof supported on iron columns. Along the lower level of the market is also a Butchers Row, with 12 small artisan shops, not so much butchers, more stained glass and hand-crafted jewellery. The Pannier Market is visible in the background of the 2018 film *The Guernsey Literary and Potato Peel Pie Society*, when nearby streets were transformed with images of swastikas and Adolf Hitler for a Nazi march.

The area to the east of the Long Bridge is East-the-Water. Chapel Park in East-the-Water was until 1969 home to the Bideford Black Mining Company. Stretching from the coast at Hartland Quay, Bideford Black is a 350-million-year-old rock strata formed from deposits of carbon, silica and aluminium oxide; often referred to as *The Mother of Coal*. The mining company refined the coal to produce Biddiblack powder, a unique pigment used as camouflage paint in the Second World War and mascara by Max Factor. The old mine entrance is still visible off Barnstaple Road, and local streets such as Mines Road, Pitt Lane and Biddiblack Way pay homage to East-the-Water's former industry.

The tarmac path ends at Bideford Station and the Bideford Railway Heritage Centre, open during school holidays and summer weekends, with a visitor centre and café in a renovated Atlantic Express carriage.

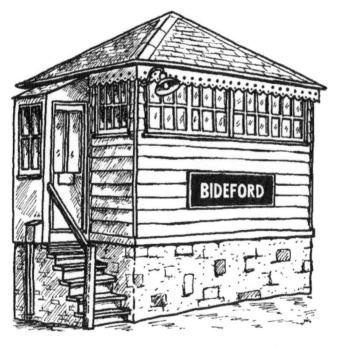

The name Bideford is thought to have derived from *by-the-ford*, in turn coming from the Welsh *bydd y ffordd*, meaning "this is the way", the way being to wade across the river at low tide.

By-the-ford now being by-the-bridge, cross the Long Bridge and turn right along the tree-lined quay. Constructed in the 16th century when Bideford was a thriving port, the original quay was used for importing Irish wool and Newfoundland cod. Upon returning from the US state of Virginia in 1586, Sir Walter Raleigh docked at the quay with a cargo that included a new recreational drug called tobacco. Legend tells that, upon seeing him smoke a pipe for the first time and fearing that he was on fire, one of Raleigh's servants doused him with water. Although tobacco was more likely first brought to these shores in 1565 by Sir John Hawkins, Raleigh did introduce the potato to Britain, which was at first treated with great suspicion.

In 1585, Richard Grenville, Lord of the Manor of Bideford and cousin to Sir Walter Raleigh, sailed to Roanoke Island off the coast of North Carolina with a seven-strong fleet carrying English settlers, with the aim of setting up a military colony on the island. Upon the return journey he captured the *Santa Maria de Vincente* and brought it back to Bideford. Eight cannons from the captured Spanish ship are in Victoria Park, north of the quay.

Returning from a similar expedition the following year, Grenville brought back a Native American, the first to set foot on English soil. In honour of his cousin, he named the Native American Raleigh. Soon after converting to Christianity, Raleigh died of flu; he is interred at Saint Mary the Virgin's Church.

Victoria Park is also home to the *Burton at Bideford* art gallery and museum. The museum has a permanent display recounting the story of Temperance Lloyd, Susannah Edwards and Mary Trembles, local women hanged for witchcraft in 1682.

Bideford is known as the *Little White Town*. The town's motto comes from author Charles Kingsley, who used the term to describe Bideford in his 1855 novel, *Westward Ho!* At the time of writing *Westward Ho!* Kingsley was living at Northdown Hall in Bideford, and with London experiencing a cholera outbreak and medical knowledge in its infancy, buildings in the town were limewashed white in the hope of preventing the spread of the disease. A statue of the author overlooks the river at the north end of the quay.

Leaving the quay, the path continues north, doing its best to hug the river's edge. It soon fails, diverting along Riverside Court to pass under Torridge Bridge before turning right to re-join the river above a low cliff. The battle continues, with further inland excursions around elegant riverside houses with their private moorings.

Speaking of battles, in the year 878 a 1,200-strong Viking army under the command of Hubba Lothbrok (son of the infamous Ragnar Lothbrok and brother of Ivar the Boneless and Sigurd Snake-in-the-Eye) set sail from south Wales aboard 23 longships. Crossing the Bristol Channel, the ships came ashore on the north Devon coast between Bideford and Appledore.

Planning to attack the Hill Fort at Kenwith, whilst marching inland the Viking army was met in a field by the Saxon army under the command of Odda, Ealdorman of Devon. As testimony to the ensuing battle, the field is now known as *Bloody Corner*. Both armies suffered heavy casualties, with Hubba and 840 of his men killed. Before the Danes retreated, it is thought that the Viking warriors were buried at Bone Hill in Northam, whilst Hubba was laid to rest under a cairn made from Lundy granite near the river at Appledore. Although the exact location of Hubba's burial cairn is uncertain, a large commemorative block of Lundy granite has since been installed on the green at Hillcliff Terrace in the seaside village.

North of Burrough Farm, the coast path crosses a dyke; at high tide, take the signed inland alternative route. The path once again diverts inland around Appledore Shipyard to join Wooda Road, leading into the village.

Follow the harbourside and continue along Irsha Street, passing Hillcliff Terrace and Appledore Lifeboat Station. Just before the garage, at low tide, turn right down the steps to cross the beach. The beach edges the Skern, a salt marsh offering rich pickings for wading birds. At high tide, join Long Lane and continue for 400 metres, turning right at the crossroads onto Burrows Lane, taking you to Northam Burrows Country Park. The Park covers 253 hectares of salt marsh, grasslands and sand dunes, a Site of Special Scientific Interest in an Area of Outstanding Natural Beauty, all included in the North Devon UNESCO Biosphere Reserve. At low tide, the Park is just 600 metres across the estuary from the sand and dunes of Braunton Burrows.

Continuing around the headland, the coast path passes landward of the dunes, skirting the fairways and bunkers of the *Royal North Devon Golf Club*; founded in 1864, the oldest golf course in England. The course is sheltered from the prevailing winds that batter Westward Ho!'s two-mile sandy beach by a pebble ridge. The ridge is formed naturally by longshore drift, with unusually large sandstone pebbles transported by the waves and underlying currents from Bideford Bay to the north.

In a tradition dating from the 19th century, locals would come together each year over the Whitsun Bank Holiday weekend in May to celebrate *Potwallopers Festival*, working together to replace the pebbles and rebuild the ridge following winter storm damage. The term *potwallopers* was first used in 1701 to describe a man eligible to vote in a parliamentary election by reason of being the head of a household in an English borough, a "household" determined by the presence of a hearth other than in a fireplace upon which a cauldron could be boiled, colloquially referred to as "walloping a pot".

Long before Westward Ho! developed, local potwallopers had the right to graze their animals on the

Burrows, in return for which they had to help rebuild the pebble ridge following the winter storms. Hence, the annual Potwallopers Festival.

The festival came and went over time until, in 2008, Natural England informed the local council that they could no longer interfere with nature to protect the Burrows and golf course as the Country Park is classified as a Site of Special Scientific Interest.

The Potwallopers Festival continues, albeit with events more aimed towards family fun than pebble ridge maintenance. And local potwallopers still retain the right to graze their animals on the Burrows.

In answer to the popular pub quiz question, Westward Ho! is the only place in the UK that's name ends with an exclamation mark! And, for a bonus point, it is also the only place in the UK named after a novel. Following the publication of *Westward Ho!* the Northam Burrows Hotel and Villa Building Company sought to promote tourism in the area by naming their new hotel after the bestselling book. Adjacent villas also took on the name, as did what is now the popular seaside village of Westward Ho!

From 1878 to 1882, Rudyard Kipling spent his early teenage years as a boarder at the United Services College in Westward Ho! Story tells that he would bunk off with his friends to the hill now known as Kipling Tors, where they would smoke cigars. Kipling's 1899 collection of short stories, *Stalky and Co.*, draws on his experiences at the college. Teddy Roosevelt, 26th President of the United States, called the novel "a story which ought never to have been written".

Continuing alongside the pebble ridge brings you to the centre of Westward Ho!, the end of today's walk and the end of the first week of trekking the South West Coast Path. Cumulative distance for the week is 87.3 miles and total ascent is 4,052 metres, just over three times the height of Ben Nevis, the UK's highest mountain.

Time for some well-deserved refreshments!

Index

163

164

165

Printed in Great Britain
by Amazon

46469814R00098